The Tiger's Fang

PAUL TWITCHELL

THE TIGER'S FANG

1st Printing — 1967

2nd Printing — 1968

3rd Printing — 1972

4th Printing — 1974

5th Printing — 1975

6th Printing — 1977

7th Printing — 1978

8th Printing — 1979

Cover Painting by Diana Stanley

For a catalogue of other books write:

ILLUMINATED WAY PRESS
P.O. Box 2449
Menlo Park, CA 94025

FOREWORD

From time to time in man's religious history, certain gifted men have set down visions of remarkable spiritual journeys. Nearly every reader will be familiar with Dante's *Divine Comedy*, John Bunyan's *Pilgrim's Progress*, and John Milton's glimpse of the heavenly hierarchy in *Paradise Lost*. These books were brilliant, allegorical descriptions of spiritual worlds that became more than personal fantasy through the creative genius of their authors. It may be that *The Tiger's Fang* is something more than another imaginative pilgrimage to a heavenly realm. *The Tiger's Fang* claims to be the record of an incredible spiritual journey that actually took place on other planes of existence.

The manuscript, according to its author, Paul Twitchell, was written with the intent of recording an experience that occurred to him while he was in the company of Rebazar Tarzs, the great Tibetan master, who is one of the leading advocates of *Eckankar*, the ancient science of soul travel.

"The book," Twitchell says, "came out of personal experience. Some will say *The Tiger's Fang* is the wild fantasy of a highly developed imagination, but one must understand that there is nothing in the world of God without some degree of truth. Even fantasy is cast out of the material cloth of God, so how can fantasy be a complete untruth? This statement should stagger the mind of man and shake the foundation of the teachings of orthodox religions, philosophies, and metaphysical concepts. However, I am prepared to make my statements out of *pure experience,* and one must remember that all experiences are unique only to the experiencers."

Whether *The Tiger's Fang* is a record of an actual spiritual journey or the vivid impression of a vision that has been granted to few mortal men, must remain a matter for the individual reader to judge. Whatever *The Tiger's Fang* may be, it is certain that the book is a most remarkable work, a volume that has few peers in its array of challenging concepts, provocative thoughts, and inspirational wisdom. It is a volume that bears repeated re-reading and careful examination. Some of the passages are not easily digested by a cursory appraisal. And some of the philosophy expressed is going to stick in the throats of the orthodox thinkers. But I predict that the almost poetic thrust of its narrative power will answer the same spiritual need among the seekers of spiritual enlightenment as Kahlil Gibran's *The Prophet.*

Paul Twitchell is the first to recognize that his book will create many diverse points of view and outright antagonisms, but he promises that the reader who approaches this book with an open mind will never be the same again.

"The entirety of God is so majestic and colossal that few in the flesh have any conception of how they might be brought closer to the Deity. We must learn to experience God through Soul. The master, or *guru,* may give one an experience of God through the emotional senses by striking the mental imagery that arouses the emotional body to great heights of ecstasy. However, the *guru* prefers that the *chela* (student) find the way by his own individual effort.

"Those Souls and spiritual travelers (the latter is the higher name for Souls who are commonly called *mahantas, gurus,* and masters), whom I know personally in the worlds beyond, have great wisdom, mercy, and compassion for all mankind, except when man becomes stubborn in his ignorance. Then they are scornful of man's unwillingness to accept what the travelers desire to teach him. Any great Soul whose spiritual mission is to help mankind, struggles under extreme hardships with man's continued refusal to weigh what is divinely presented to him."

According to Paul Twitchell, *The Tiger's Fang* is one such divine presentation. A presentation which resulted from the concern of a spiritual traveler, Rebazar Tarzs, who desired to reveal certain cosmic truths to his *chela*, Paul Twitchell. A spiritual traveler of the caliber of Rebazar Tarzs does not care whether we accept him or his words, Twitchell tells us, but he does desire that we listen, weigh, and judge what he says.

"Here is the crux of the matter," Twitchell explains. "If we listen, weigh, and judge the wisdom of the living ECK master, we shall never again be the same. The spiritual traveler addresses the Soul, not the mind nor the body; and he awakens the Soul to its true destiny."

Whether or not such a revelation occurs to one who picks up *The Tiger's Fang* for serious study, depends, of course, upon the individual reader. But, as Paul Twitchell promises, those readers who accompany him with an open mind will probably never be quite the same again.

Brad Steiger
October, 1968

"Man does not know real freedom. His dogmas are set and imposed upon him from the outside; his religious beliefs become frozen over the centuries. They do not come from within, anymore. They belong to an outside world."

Niranjan: The Tiger's Fang

Introduction

This manuscript was written with the idea of re-cording an experience that occured to me, while in the presence of Rebazar Tarzs, the great Tibetan saint, who is the leading advocate of Eckankar, the ancient science of Soul Travel.

The book came out of personal experience. What is written on these pages is not as important as the recording of those worlds that few Souls, other than the saints, have ever visited.

Some will say this book is the wild fantasy of a highly developed imagination, but one must understand that there is nothing in the world of God without some degree of truth. Even fantasy is cast out of the material cloth of God, so how can fantasy be a complete untruth?

This statement should stagger the mind of man and shake the foundation of the teachings of orthodox religions, philosophies, and metaphysical concepts. However I am prepared to make my statements out of pure experience and one must remember that all experiences are unique only to the experiencer.

The entirety of God is so majestic and colossal that none of the flesh, and few in the other worlds, have any conception that might bring them closer to the Deity. We do not, and cannot, know God. We must experience Him through Soul, and this body is so close to the mind that one can hardly distinguish one from the other, except in the final experience.

A teacher, or guru, may give you an experience of God through the emotional senses by striking the mental imagery that arouses the emotional body to great heights of ecstasy. However this is not likely for he prefers that you find the way by your own individual effort. So the guru will usually tell you how, and point to all the ways, via the experiences in God, that you are striving to reach.

This book should make history along certain lines of spiritual knowledge. However, it will create many diverse points of view, namely curiosity, inspiration and antagonism.

It is only right to tell you that all books, in their endeavor to explain God, also do this. No two readers, out of the depth of their understanding and experience, would hardly agree with this statement. If they do, it becomes a fact known as reality. Disagreement leaves the explanation in the realm of mystery and unreality.

Those Souls and spiritual travelers (the latter is the higher name for Souls who are commonly called teachers, gurus, and masters), whom I know personally from the worlds beyond, have great wisdom, mercy and compassion for all mankind except when man becomes stubborn in his ignorance. Then they are scornful of man's unwillingness to accept what the travelers desire to teach him. It really is not in the act of doing for him which has brought them to this attitude in relationship with man, but any great Soul whose spiritual mission is to help mankind, struggles under extreme hardships with the continued refusal of man to weigh what is divinely presented to him.

No spiritual traveler really cares a hoot whether we accept him or his words but he does desire that we listen, weigh and judge what he says. Here is the catch of the thing. For if we listen, weigh and judge his wisdom then his words are planted in us and we shall never again be the same. I rightfully state that we become "A Hound of Heaven," as Francis Thompson so aptly titled his little book.

When a traveler speaks, we, in ignorance, think he speaks to the physical self. This is wrong. He addresses the Soul, not the mind nor the body, and awakens the Soul to its true destiny.

There is danger in this however. If the person is not normally experienced in the world of spirit he may be contacted by one with only psychic powers, and awaken within him those lower faculties. We often mistake psychic awareness for that of the spiritual. This is not good for it stops our growth on the spiritual path.

I repeat again that if you read this book with an open mind you will never be the same again. I can guarantee this for you.

Good reading to you.

Paul Twitchell

CHAPTERS

CHAPTER 1

Sailors of the Cosmic Sea

an has always had the consuming desire to sail the cosmic seas and eventually reach the far shores where dwells the Lord of All Creation. So it is that Rebazar Tarzs, one who has finished the voyage, seeks to see that others might have the same opportunity.

As one who has had the experience of this voyage and returned to life in this world, many conclusions have been reached and recorded. In fact we believe what we want to believe and the reading of any sacred scripture will not bring one any closer to God. It is entirely up to the individual to advance himself in understanding. No one, not even a spiritual traveler, will give us the understanding. We are furnished only with the opportunity.

The study of sacred scriptures, singing of hymns and the seeking of God, as well as the constant talking about God, only increases the appetite of the senses to enjoy themselves in search for the Almighty One. These, in themselves, do not bring the seeker any closer to God, only the experiencing of God is important and does bring the seeker closer.

Before delving into this subject too deeply I wish to make clear that the descent of spirit into the human consciousness will bring liberation from the excessive control of human and physical forces in one's life. This force, however, is an essential part of ourselves. Make no mistake about that! And it is this force with which we must contend as long as we are a part of the dual worlds. More important, we should not make any separation of these forces for both are God. They need one another as long as we are creating the worlds below the Second Grand Division.

Secondly, I wish to point out that the human form is the focal point for the energies of this world, and serves as a point of balance between them. All that are material substances, foods and water, are of the negative nature; and all that is breath, atoms, electrons, and prana vitality, are of the positive nature. We cannot do without either as long as we are here on this earth in human embodiment.

As the experiencer, all that one experiences is reality, but to the rest of the world it may not be that simple because none of us hardly have the same experiences subjectively. All cosmic experiences, however, follow a similar pattern as do objective experiences on the earth plane. A spiritual traveler, who is a spiritual psychologist, can easily see what your problems are by a glance at your physical form and face. He need not be concerned with looking at an aura, or listening to your problems. If he desires to help, it will be done, or, you may be left alone to solve any obstacles.

This leads us into the main topic of experience. We are all sailors of the cosmic seas, in our little selves serving as boats, trying to sail toward that distant shore. And this begins the revelation of my experience.

• • •

One evening I lay down in a hotel room in Srinagar in hopes that the following morning contact would be made with a Rishi, who lived nearby in an Ashram, but was almost inaccessible to those like myself seeking some experience with God.

Almost as quickly as my eyes were closed I awoke in the Atma Sarup, or what is known as the Soul body, to find myself walking along a sandy beach where the wild surf lashed the shore and a wind whipped the pines along the edge of the strand.

There were pale, white clouds in an azure sky. Something about the landscape was ethereal and my pulse was quickened with the thought that this was an out-of-the-body projection via the dream technique. The color, the invigorating air and the beauty were beyond words. It seemed as if there was God in Everything.

I felt no fear at this sudden transportation but curiosity, tugging at my mind, asked the question of where was I? Somewhere in the back of my mind it seemed that this was not a strange place after all... that sometime, in the afterworlds, in the earlier travels with Rebazar Tarzs, I had gone through this section of landscape. But a peaceful feeling settled over me, and all was accepted for what it was.

The sea was crystal blue and the lacy surf was like a million sparkling diamonds that dashed up against the sandy beach and ran off into the sea again.

The distance was majestic with foaming whitecaps. Yet there was a silence, a strange, wonderful silence so deep reaching that it stirred through me. Looking down at my body a feeling of joy went through me, I was wearing a white robe of light which flowed around in a circular motion in a gentle swirling current. There were no feet, no hands, nothing but a ball of swirling light. My vision was below where my feet should have been and it was also in back of the head. It was anywhere I directed my attention... all simultaneously. When I spoke there was a multitude of sounds issuing from me.

A brilliant sphere of light appeared on the horizon and as it came closer and grew larger it revealed itself as a small sailing vessel, at the tiller was Rebazar Tarzs.

He was a solid man with coal black eyes and a strong, square face. His hair was clipped closely to his head and he wore a dark, wine colored robe which was held to his body with a small belt-like rope.

He guided the craft to shore and waved for me to board it then together we turned back to the sea again. As we glided over the rough water he leaned over the side and spoke.

"This is the cosmic sea of life," he explained. "Look at the water. It is not really water as you think it may be, but the trillions of undeveloped Souls struggling to find their way to God perfection. Look!"

I could see the miniature lights, millions upon millions of them, like the light of Soul within which both Rebazar Tarzs and myself were wrapped, moving through the waters, of what I believed first was the sea. Yet I saw they composed the sea itself, and although crystal clear to the vision they were compact like water, forever moving into the worlds, moving from somewhere to somewhere else.

"The ocean of love and mercy," said Rebazar Tarzs. "The love current which I often speak of as the Master Power, is always moving into the worlds, into that vast area beyond, into space, time and motion. That which comprises the worlds below the Second Grand Division!"

Looking about I found that we seemed to be completely in a mighty ocean, which was like the air itself, blue in nature and yet marvelously clear as if in the earth world. We were sailing toward a landfall in the distance and yet it seemed not far away, only at the fingertips.

Soon I saw a city surrounded by a high wall, so

4

high it reached the clouds. Behind the wall was a gigantic mountain, the likes of which no one has ever seen before. Its heights could have been greater than Mount Everest, many times over and out of its summit poured lights, millions of lights, flowing into the worlds, onward and onward into the clear sky until they faded in the light of a majestic sun.

Rebazar Tarzs said, "That is the great mountain of Sahasra-dal-Kanwal. Sometimes it is called the mountain of light. Look closely and you will see a thousand varied lights clustered around one huge central light, each in the form of a gigantic lotus flower. This is the powerhouse of the physical universe which we call Pinda, that of the physical worlds. From this gigantic dynamo flows all the power that creates and sustains all the entire creations below it, worlds upon worlds without end.

"That is the city of Sahasra-dal-Kanwal, the capital of the astral world," said the Tibetan. "We will stop here to gather enlightenment and knowledge from the ruler of this world, Jot Niranjan, who is the manifestation of all negative power in this universe; the king over all the Pinda world, which includes the physical universe and Anda, the second grand division.

"This corresponds with the thousand petalied lotus of which we speak so much in the physical body and the universe of the Pinda represents the physical body of man. So you see it is a fact that you never leave yourself. That robe which you believe is a ball of light turns out only to be your Soul body."

We left the boat at the wharf and walked up a street with white walls on either side. Everything seemed to be made of soft, white stone that glistened in the reddish light of a sun which was not visible to the eye. There were round, white domes peering over the high walls like oriental temples and everywhere people walked in strident, joyful steps, heads lifted

5

with eyes sparkling as though life was completely blissful. From somewhere came the sounds of beautiful music. Overhead were strange square shaped objects flying through the sky.

"Another version of the flying saucers," Rebazar Tarzs smiled. "I suppose that we call them flying squares. They come from the lowest division of the cosmic universe, that we call Pinda, the physical worlds."

He added, "They come out of the Sun-Worlds and Moon-Worlds, using a form of cosmic energy which is very simple, though man seems to be struggling with the idea of transforming the atom into ordinary energy. The zone of Ashta-dal-Kanwal, which is the pure astral zone between these worlds where you meet with my light body, is of importance to the space people, especially the mystics of their worlds."

He added, "There are very few psychics who have actually penetrated beyond the bowels of the Astral world. Suppose that you lived in the gloom of the earth's center and entered large caves where there was some light, but not complete light. Wouldn't you believe this was heaven, even though the people there were not completely happy?"

"Then if you got out of the earth's bowels into a bright sunlit city you would actually believe it was Paradise. The same comparison lies between the earth world and the top of the astral world."

The beings that passed us were beautiful, more beautiful than I had ever seen before. Their youth was like that of the Greek gods, dressed in short white tunics and busy with some creative art work. Rebazar Tarzs explained that none in this world actually worked at commercial occupations but all sought out some form of art to develop their character through creative work which was exchanged in great quantities throughout this universe. He had previously said there

6

were many beings living in this world who were famous in earth history, though I had never seen any during my previous trips here.

A dog trotted by and disappeared into a tree. The Tibetan explained this was the world of thought where all things existed in temporary abode, subject to thought action. The dog appeared on the other side and trotted away. The Lama explained that this was magic and he was responsible for the working of the phenomena for my benefit.

To give me further proof he showed me beings walking past, on their hands, upside down, carrying packages with their feet. He laughed and then explained that it was only an illusion thrown before my vision. The world rightened again and I saw clearly what had happened. He continued saying it was a part of the maya (illusion) on this plane, and it was stronger here than on the earth plane because thought power was greater.

He was only debunking the power of vision to see and create attitudes which we gain by wrong conception.

We went through this lovely city which defies verbal description. Near the center we saw the wide beautiful boulevards converging upon a circle so huge that it would easily have been described as fifty to a hundred thousand miles in circumference. In the center of the circle stood a statue of a colossal figure, with its head in the clouds; so huge that my eyes could not see the head. It could have taken days to encircle the legs which stood sprawled like the old statue of Rhodes that overlooked the world in the ancient days.

"This is a statue representing and honoring the ruler of the lower planes, Jot Niranjan," the Tibetan said. "Although the people of this world live for thousands of years which gives them a sense of being immortal no one knows when this statue was erected. It came from an ancient race that came out of the dim, misty history of the astral world. This race was called the Seres, a mighty host of beings that explored all the lower worlds leaving traces on the Earth planets. You do not read or hear of them, only occasionally there is a report of finding bones of skeletons which must have been eighteen to twenty feet tall of some unknown race of men on earth. These people were the fathering tribe of the Lemurians and Atlanteans. Many of the planetary groups come from the Seres, especially the space people. They have superior knowledge and occult powers.

"I want you to see another sight which is on our way to Jot Niranjan's castle."

Taking my hand we soared upward over the great city. He pointed out the Temple of Golden Wisdom where a number of spiritual travelers, including himself, taught disciples on this plane. The museum of the astral world was nearby and the flowering gardens of Zrephs was gorgeous to behold. Many paradises of religions and cults of the minority groups have their heavenly abode in this region. They believe that this is the highest they can achieve in their afterlife.

We came to the Mountain of Light. So bright were the gigantic streams of light pouring out of its top, like a volcano crater, that I could hardly look at it. These lights were so enormous pouring into the worlds of this universe that words cannot describe them. They were varied colors, roaring through the ethers in unnamed sounds. This was the powerhouse of the physical and astral worlds. It reminded me of the Cave of Eternal Flame in Rider Haggard's book, "She." What was shown to me is beyond the scope of a verbal description; I would not ever attempt it. This is the center of creation for the subtle and physical worlds.

We passed through these lights without harm. I saw

the ethereal images of the huge planetary spirits moving through the lights, going about their various duties. We were then walking through a hall filled with soft, indirect lights that poured out in bouyant energies. The ceilings were filled with fresco paintings of some far distant past races.

We sped on, not stopping to examine any of the murals which the spiritual traveler explained briefly were the history of the Seres races. Suddenly we were standing inside a vast room. I cannot tell you if it was a room or not, for there seemed to be a sky overhead, and stars shining like diamonds upon this huge, dark bowl of space.

An entity sat upon a dais in the center of the bowl. Two large candles flickered on each side of this being who was clad in a light red robe. Blazing eyes watched us keenly from out of narrow slits set in a broad cheek boned face whose deeply chiseled features were as immobile as if they belonged to a bronze statue.

"The Lord of This World," explained Rebazar Tarzs, bowing. "He has manifested himself to greet us. Usually he lives in the invisible as pure negative nature itseif."

Niranjan laughed contemptuously. "You come Godman, again, to see my throne. You who knows all, and lives in the pure spirit of He that is all, bring now a traveler who seeks nothing."

"He is traveling with me to the true kingdom, my Lord!" Rebazar Tarzs replied.

"You speak in riddles calling me, Lord. You speak only to thyself, for concerning the creation of any object, it is for you to speak. I am both sublime and dull. This is like lewdness in the cathedral.

"Listen travelers, I can tell you all and nothing. Whosoever says love conquers all is wrong. Almost everything conquers love, or attempts it. There is nothing, so seek nothing for it will bring you all you desire, and I can tell that such desires are illusionary for you are in my grasp. I will not let you leave until divine mind understanding enters into your being.

"Travelers, your finer body manifests itself in realms invisible to the human eye. Your intellect penetrates deeper than your senses. Every visible fact in connection with the body is an undertone of invisible facts or processes; every organ, every body function you study is but the effects of higher functions from out of this world, and the worlds beyond.

"Your preachers know nothing; your philosophers are little better and your thinkers on the earth plane are even worse. You talk with one another, make your pretty speeches about character, courage, honor, et cetera. You see romance where it does not exist — or if it does exist, it exists in bloody and sorrowful depths that you cannot fathom.

"This readily sums up man's findings.

"Man has conquered the earth planet with his physical sciences and now reaches out to other planets and into space. What good have the teachers done for you? Those few who have spiritual insight have been mocked and destroyed.

"Your world is sick, more sick that it has ever been and man is responsible for this. Wisdom is never for the multitudes, but for the few who seek it.

"Some call me God, not knowing the divine Truth, for having seen my form in light they believe they have come to the ultimate end. But they do not seek Truth. What they would call the divine powers are not sought for as mediums toward the greater understanding of ultimate reality but only as development for their own sake.

"The world you live in is but an ashcan and those who serve there to help man always go back knowing that they will be met with scorn and cruelty.

"In your search for supreme enlightenment, the

10

teachers, whose ignorance is often appalling, try to make you reach this end by observing moral precepts, righteous living, compassion and spiritual achievement. I as the Supreme Lord of this World, however, tell you that it is more than the seeking of such attributes of God.

"You must find clever techniques for spiritual attainments, make many psychic experiments and acquire the supernormal powers.

"Few in the world of the earth planet understand, except for the spiritual travelers who are hidden from the eyes of the profane masses. Those who talk openly or write books or preach philosophies cannot tell you anything — nor teach anything to the peoples of the worlds. Their ignorance is appalling.

"What true teacher cares whether you listen to him or not? None! These travelers do not seek out man to teach him. The spark of divine wisdom must be lit in man's heart and arouse him to look for God — to look for the teacher.

"The Occidental mystics are wrong in their techniques to reach God and most of the Orientals are also wrong. Yet they will tell you that they, and they alone, are right and will defend their attitude and statement of facts to the death.

"The Occidental mystic searching for God has to tear himself away from the physical world. On the way to the Sugmad, the Supreme Reality, he has to travel across this world of astral forces or the psychic universe. If you have a true spiritual traveler for a teacher he will show you everything including the psychic techniques to acquire super powers, and the true tests for spiritual and psychic experiments. He will also show you an insight into the psychic and spiritual matters which will be far beyond anything you can learn in a multitude of incarnations. Only a

Godman, like yourself, can give one this insight into all things.

"A large part of the spiritual science is so transcendental that it cannot be put into words and is communicated from a traveler to man by means of telepathy. That is why much of it, the sublime Truths, are never actually put upon paper or even spoken orally.

"Remember that knowledge of divine Truth is not a thing you can read about in books, discuss with others, or even hear told. It is a thing you must experience alone. Not even a Godman will take part in this experience, for it is the road upward to eternity and to Godhood itself. Therefore you must travel it alone, under the vigil of a spiritual traveler, says Rebazar Tarzs, here, or by you, in your own way.

"Man does not know real freedom. His dogmas are set and imposed upon him from the outside; his religious beliefs become frozen over the centuries. His religions do not come from within, anymore. They belong to an outside world.

"The true teachings never come from the outside, but have to grow from within, under the guidance and with the help of the spiritual travelers. The truth never pretends it has the monopoly on God. There are many ways to God, and each Soul must be free to choose which one he prefers. Earth climates, geography, races and psychic conditions are responsible for the growth of its religions. These philosophies adapt themselves to the emotional needs of their devotees and each is basically as good as the other.

"Each of the Occidential philosophies and religions pretend that theirs alone and individually is the true church, but they have not grown alongside their own physical sciences. There is a gap between spiritual science and physical science which will never be closed until man learns to accept both into his social being.

"The worldly scientists and philosophers have tried to deny the reality of the spiritual world, and sought refuge in a dreary mass of materialism which is tragic. But it serves my purpose for I am the creator of this universe and there must always be my three sides of nature: birth, survival and death.

"And seeing the increasing chaos within the physical universe I have not hesitated to tell you this.

"I pass you further into the next world for there are many interesting aspects of the divine nature of God. Hardly any of it is new to you but nevertheless there is always something to enlighten one for greater understanding."

CHAPTER 2

The Road to Sat Lok

So far I cannot describe the chaos of atoms in the other worlds at the points of creation, and there are many many points of creation in the three lower worlds through which Rebazar Tarzs and I had to pass in order to reach the rim of the Second Region.

This second plane is called the Brahmanda plane. It is known to all travelers by the name of its overlord, Brahm. Many worship this deity as the supreme being of all creation.

Generally speaking, of those who have had the experience of movement of Soul body have never traveled anywhere outside the three worlds nor, for a fact, within the three worlds either. This statement means that we do not travel anywhere once outside matter, energy, space and time.

However, the experience of the inner journey is unique. The initiate of any spiritual traveler never travels in the astral body. The traveler makes very little use of the astral body of anyone, but makes Soul partake in its experience for the sake of learning that this is a means to the end and not an end for the means. How can you travel anywhere outside of space, time and causation? All there is is eternity and all is not in eternity. The body, mind and Soul is always in eternity and all is now, this moment — this instance. That which is called space, time and motion is born of the mind and this includes the lower creation.

Therefore, space, time and motion is only an aspect of the three worlds below the Second Grand Division. This includes the physical, astral, and mental worlds — — all of which are within this universe of the three universes, and within the mind of man. These are the sheathings which man has within himself and he can, in a way of saying, travel within these sheaths to experience psychic phenomena. This is one of the disadvantages of being without a true teacher. When one goes in the opposite direction with psychic study, then he is worse off than the one who knows nothing.

Only a spiritual traveler can safely take a Soul through these planes to God, unless Soul has already experienced journeys within its own sheathings. This explains why so many who start out on the path become entangled in their own nature. Their way is lost and they appeal to their teacher for help — but, not being a true spiritual traveler he cannot lift his hand to help because he lacks the power or the knowledge to untangle them from the deep mire into which they have sunk.

There is a dire need for every Soul to first seek a spiritual traveler. Few on this earth plane are experienced in psychic phenomena. Maya will trap them invariably. Even those who were fully confident in their own ability have not escaped Maya. The greatest of cosmic travelers, Jesus, Buddha, and others, have been caught up in the web of this wonderful weaver of dreams. And what wonderful dreams this lady of Maya can weave around one. They are more beautiful than any spell cast by drugs.

* * *

We arrived at that glorious city of Kailash, capital of this magnificent plane. The first sight of it is breathtaking and staggering to the imagination for it is the very place that St. John called in his revelations, the Holy City of Jerusalem, which lay foursquare and the length is as large as the breadth. The length, height and breadth were equal he said, and so is this city.

Kailash rests at the foot of three towering peaks; Mer, Sumer, and Kailash, that are higher than the Mountain of Light in the astral world. These are mountains of grandeur, soaring so high that the eyes strain for sight of their heads. The peaks are partly hidden by vast streams of the light of creation pouring from their distant heights.

This is the top of the three worlds and is the highest region known to most religions including Christianity. Its ruler, Brahma, is supposed to be the Supreme Being for all Indian religions.

This is the home of Mohammed and his God, Allah; Krishna, Buddha and other religious leaders. Their heavens are established on this plane, near the city of Kailash. It is always the city of God to them — — where they have established their heavenly paradise.

The heavenly light is glorious! The color of the light is coppery and spreads over the vast deserts, mountains and gardens where dwells a happy race of people who live on a street that runs through little brook beds, from a central river known to many as the river of Jordon, or by other names in various religions.

This city is on the edge of an ocean the likes of which you have never experienced. It appears to be like smooth glass and you would think so unless trying to step on it.

This plane is controlled by Brahma whose chief duty is to supervise the great power called AUM — the function of which, as a part of the great sound current, is to create, maintain and destroy the universes below this region. This is the creation of creations of the material and mind worlds. Many of the great scriptures have sprung from this region, including the Vedas.

The negative current which splits off the AUM power is called Shakti, or the Mother Energy. In Indian philosophy this is the creative mother who married Brahm and has three offsprings, Vishnu, Shiva and Brahma. They are: Brahma, who creates; Vishnu, who preserves; and Shiva, who destroys.

The city is beautiful and has a wall adorned with all manner of precious stones. Like John's description in his Revelations this wall is made up of twelve foundations, and each, starting from the bottom upward has the following precious stones: jasper, sapphire, chalcedony, emerald, sardonyx, sardius, topaz, chrysoprasus, jacinth and amethyst.

There are twelve gates of pearl and the streets and city buildings are of pure gold, similar to clear glass. It needs no sun for the very light which pours from the city lightens the whole region. The light which is the very sound of AUM, comes from a great tunnel under the three mountains.

We entered a gate and walked into the city where people who appeared like angels were engaged in some spiritual duties. The Tibetan pointed out their various duties which were not for themselves but for the worlds to which they belonged. The writing of books, the painting of arts, sculpturing, and the advancement in sciences of the material worlds.

"There is no night here," said Rebazar Tarzs, "It is a place where only the wise can enter. It is the home of the Universal Mind Power. See for yourself for there is the book of life and the works going into it."

There was an angel, so mammoth that words have no description, writing in an enormous book miles upon miles in length, width and thickness. The pages were being flipped rapidly; erasing when a Soul left the material world by death, and writing down when a Soul was reincarnated again. Smiling, the beautiful face of this angel was so intriguing that it took Rebazar Tarzs' touch to turn me again to the present.

He took me to the River of Light that was pouring from the foot of the mountains, which, in all theology we know as the throne of God. Its light moves constantly outward into space, time and eternity, into the three worlds beyond — — creating, maintaining and destroying all there is. The word IS — and GOD DOES, is simplified when you see this magnificient River of Light.

God, Brahm, the Lord of this world sits upon his throne at the fountainhead, the source of this river, in the midst of the mountain peaks. The stream came bubbling, leaping and running joyously from out of the foot of the throne, behind him.

He was a majestic light. This is about the extent of words to describe this deity. I don't know how to describe what this gigantic, this two hundred or maybe five hundred foot of Soul looks like. He is pure light with only a face showing, no other features of limbs, arms, or body. That face was so startlingly like Rebazar Tarzs that I was stunned into silence.

The voice that speaks from it is magnificent, a glorious AUM rolling, a drum of thunder that pierces the air and shatters the heart. All the room shakes with a trembling as if an earthquake rocks it.

19

"I am Brahm!" it said with gusto, an awe-inspiring command that to listen was to be on holy terms with the Almighty. "I am Brahm, the Lord of the Worlds. There is no other but myself! Love me for myself and none other. Become mine, enter into my heart and see the pure light of God, for I am God and there is no other beyond me, nor any behind me. I am It, and I am He! Look upon my face!

"This is the face of God! See pilgrims of the Holy Grail! See, I can speak and give life to all. Seek nothing but me, and I will give you back only that which you give me! My law is the balanced scales of life!

"God is dead, for I am God. Truth is simple. Balance is simple. Rhythmic balanced interchanges between all poles of opposite expression in God, is the consummate art of God's universe of light.

"Understand this and you will understand the one fundamental law of my universe which shows you where lies the balanced continuity of all creative expression in my electric wave universe of two conditioned lights in seething motion.

"This law records my Oneness into an idea of creation which divides into countless seemingly separate parts of that Whole which is myself only. The Ideal. The Idea and God.

"No Soul should seek any further pilgrimage for this is the end of the journey!" The great eyes twinkled and took on a majestic sterness. "You have met God, who is myself. I penetrate all things with the Universal Mind Power. I am he who is the Soul of all. You are in me and I am in you. Be not deceived for this is the ultimate of all goals in the spiritual kingdom.

"Rest yourself in my arms. I will give you peace and comfort. I will bring the Saviors, countless ones to the worlds below, to give man the Holy Science.

"Hear my voice. It is within every man ceaselessly whispering for Soul to arouse itself. Every desire written in man's heart is carried into the heart of hearts — my heart. But few are there who ask in reverence, and still fewer who hear my voice.

"What man mistakes for thinking is but an electric awareness of things sensed and recorded within the brain cells for repetitive usage through memories.

"Memories have no relation to knowledge of Universal Mind which is in man, these memories of course are no more than an electrical machine. What man thinks of as a living body is but an electrically motivated machine which simulates life through motion extended to it from its center, Soul which alone lives and wills the body into movement from my commands.

"Man is not free. No man is free under my rulership for I am everywhere and doing all things, at all times. You are my subjects and I will hold you within my grasp throughout eternity!"

His thunderous laughter boomed through the mountains electrifying the walls and shaking the great peaks.

"Man is forever seeking My Light. And when he finds it becomes transformed.

"And as you find it you gradually find the Soul of My divine Self, which is the light!

"As you become more and more transformed by the God-light of the awakening Soul within you, you leave the jungle of the earth world further below in darkness.

"Man cannot bear much of the light at a time because his physical being is still new and too near the jungle of materiality. All who are well out of that jungle have already found enough of my light to illumine their way from its dark depths.

"You cannot for one moment remove your seeking

eyes from my heaven, for ever so slight a glimpse below into the dark brings you back into the fear of the dark which tempts you to plunge into it again.

"Look for me then, forever upward in this high heaven of light where glory awaits the fearless, the courageous Souls, all knowing seekers of beauty in the purity of my light.

"If your eyes are in my heavens, the light will shine forever in you and you will be transformed as you find it ever widening in your vision.

"When all mankind has found my light, the play of Maya will be finished. Also your planet will be finished as a house for mankind. It will then be pushed off its ever expanding path, destroyed by fire so no life force can live upon it in flesh form and will become a cold orbit to circle in the space of the lower universe. Venus moving gradually into position will become the stage for the next repetition of the ascent of man in the solar system.

"This is happening in every solar system in my universes below this world of Universal Mind.

"Poetry is the only language which can reflect any understanding between spirit and man. Use poetry for all occasions when speaking of me, thy God!

"As the moon shines serenely in the sky, casting its reflections in countless places so my light shines upon all worlds. Nothing is outside my body, the light of the worlds below. Not even the reflected shadow is beyond my being.

"All shadows of the earth moon are as numerous as the bodies of man, but none is different from another, nor has the moon left its position in the sky by any means.

"Good and evil, ugly and beautiful are my virtues. Nothing can deprive me of them. I love because it is my nature; I snare man because it is my nature, and

22

I hate man because it is my nature, and I preserve life because it is my nature.

"Man is curious about this. But I will not tell him; that is my nature. I am the essence of divine science of the truth, but like any scientist of the earth world, I do not tell why things happen as they do. You can put a formula together and get music from the ethers but the average homo sapiens does not know why. So be it in this world, people must love and obey but I will never explain to them the reason.

"To think is to create. This is why this is the highest plane, and to create one must do so with light. There is nothing that is not light and sound.

"When I think, ideas are born. The light registers my idea in the twin lights of sex beings, of my thinking, and a form is born in the image of my thought.

"Oh ho, then you know that I am He who gives life to man. There can be no other, although you are taught so, from some who believe they have reached the higher life.

"Worship me, love me, and give up everything for my love. Then perhaps I can return that love to you. But you must desire me, love me, and give all to me. Suffer for my cause, make the supreme sacrifice for my love. If it is enough then I will return everything a hundred fold, otherwise nothing will come to you.

"I can give you nothing if you have no desire for me. I am the Supreme Being in all my worlds, remember this — in all my worlds. This is correct and absolute. The God of all Gods! Nothing else here is higher than me!

"I never change, nor do I evolve. It is the mind of man that evolves and comes into understanding of my divine reality. Man is the worm that becomes the serpent. Man's piltdown culture will never last; his intense search for my divine reality has become a worldliness which is astounding to the Gods of the lesser worlds.

"None can help you until the desire for Me is greater than anything else. Come be my own, let yourself live within Me and let my happiness be your happiness. You need nothing but my love."

I looked at Rebazar Tarzs who spread his hands and shrugged. "This is the way maya works. It tries to tell you that this, whatever it represents is the ultimate of the real goal. If it's art, that is the last and fullest of all arts, and if it's marriage, that is the end of all. If it is Brahm, then he is the end of all things.

"Every Soul must be free to think and act and to grant all other Souls these abilities. An Avatar will never tell you what to do with your life."

Brahm spoke again in his great voice. "I create my imaged body with the inbreathing of my pulsing universe within myself. This world is my imagination, but my imagination is not me, only the shadow of me. Therefore all things are the shadows, or the images, but they are not me, although I am in them and they are in me.

"Nothing can exist without me, for nothing has existence, except through form. Then these do not exist for they are not me. I exist alone: I am the existing Father; the All in All.

"Man's mind cannot grasp this. I am the light and Mind. Mind is light and myself. How can man understand this? Mind knows and mind thinks what it knows, so therefore mind thinks in opposite directions simultaneously projecting through end opposing end and subsequently repeating in cycles. These ends are the lights which are known as positive and negative, both needed to create form -- to crystallize my forms in the worlds of duality.

"My inner mind is always still. This is the form of creation which exists within my worlds. My thinking and imagining are the qualities of the knowledge of this inner mind, which is timeless and stillness. Likewise know that man's mind with its thinking and imagining is as timeless and still as mind in myself.

"Stillness never can be motion, or become motion, but it always appears to be motion. Motion merely seems, but stillness always is. The balance in the universal worlds can never be other than their own balance but always seem to be in motion, or tipping the scales.

"There is nothing but rest in the whole worlds of my kingdom. Illusion which is motion springs from stillness of mind and returns to stillness, always does, never fails. Man must watch his mind constantly.

"This mind knows but one fact that its own idea of creation is the whole. But mind thinks this singular whole into seemingly many parts. So the illusion of motion which we call creation, and the illusion of substance which is called matter are opposite. Not even the ground upon which you stand is solid and far less solid than any earthly ground. The vibrations are higher and finer, and so is the mental body which is worn here giving the same illusion as being in the earthly body.

"All earth philosophers have been those who loved the mind philosophies and not the God philosophy — all except the Saints who come from out of the House of God, a mysterious race of people that give teaching to the few who can understand. You might call them the Spiritual Travelers.

"From where do these Spiritual Travelers come? Despite what the teachings are, most all true travelers are men. But I will leave this for another to explain, for I have other things to tell you.

25

"It is this. Matter, motion, time, change, dimension and substance has no existence. The light of the knower, in the pure mind, alone exists.

"This explains that there is but one mind and one thinker!

"This is completely true in my world for nothing else could exist because the mind is none other than myself. So bow down to my greatness.

"The one light of the self is the Soul of God. It is the universal Soul which centers all omnipresent self-creating bodies of God Souls. This self-creating universe is the Mind-imaged body of myself, and record of my whole thinking.

"Man cannot know my body but you can see it in all things. Likewise man cannot know himself. What I am, man is. Myself and man are one, but I am the greatest of all creators. None are greater than I.

"There are other worlds besides mine which have finer vibrations and that which you call higher than mine, upward on the road to the true heavens but none of them, meaning their rulers have the power of Creation. And that is why I am unique and different. I am the creator, the greatest of creators outside God, and that is why I am God and why I am worshipped as God. That is why all religions have set me up as God. They do not know any different, for they cannot truly understand God. They only understand creation through the mind-senses.

"Therefore, I am a manifestation of all things within these dual worlds, but still I am the mind power that has the right to rule and give birth, maintain and destroy. What ruler can do that? None unless I command them to do so.

"Man lives in two universes, instead of one! The magnetic mind universe of knowing and the moving thought of mind-rhythmic-wave universe of sensing.

"You cannot sense the magnetic universe of God's knowing nor can you know the electric-wave universe of my thinking. The true mind-universe of the one light of all-knowing is all that is. The vibrating electric wave universe of sensing merely seems to be illusion.

"The one still light which you contact in meditation is the Light of God, the Master Power, the Christ Consciousness or whatever you desire to call it, that which watches over all creating things at countless points locatably by man, but nevertheless invisible to him.

"This light is completely still. It neither attracts nor repels. You must know the nature and the purpose of the opposite poles of light, negative and positive, the earth and heaven of Sat Lok, the true home of the Sugmad, or what you call God on earth.

"You must realize that the power lies within the stillness of Soul and not in the motion by means of which you manifest that stillness. You must know that Soul is God, or myself, within you. Also you must know that gradually the dawning awareness of this light of mine is you, for it comes as the awareness of your purpose in both manifesting the light and the power to manifest it at will.

"Man must come to know the universe of my body for what it is instead of what his senses have made him believe.

"Man must know that this forever-creating universe of mind and matter which seems so real to him is but a cosmic motion picture, conceived by myself. It is but an electrical picture play, of cause and effect thrown on the black screen of imaged space and time.

"The cause is real. The effect is but a simulation of the reality -- the shadow of the real.

"Soul or self, of man is cause. His self-creating

body is effect. The universe of light and sound are static.

"My perpetually creating electric-wave world of two moving lights is dynamic. It moves forever. The two moving lights are projected through one another from the static. One, to create illusion of the idea that they must manifest. The illusion which manifests the idea of creation through seeming motion is not the idea which it seemingly manifests.

"Creation is the product of mind-knowing expressed in form by mind-thinking. The product of mind is not the idea which is simulated, no idea of mind created it, but it is simulated by form and motion. Idea is eternal and belongs to my static universe of knowing.

"The form of an idea is transient but is eternally repeated as transient forms of the idea. Thus the foundation of the spiritual universe is stillness; the balanced state of the One magnetic light of God. And this being so then man should be well aware that balanced static, or balanced stillness is the positive principle of stability and unity.

"Therefore on one hand the foundation of the physical universe motion; the ever-changing motion arising out of pairs of unbalanced conditions which must forever move to seek the balanced stillness of unity from which they have sprung as a multiple pair of units. There is no negative, or reactive here.

"Unbalanced motion is the negative or reactive principle of instability, multiplicity and separateness which is this physical universe of electric octave waves of opposing lights.

"There is no positive in the negative principle. It is composed entirely of pairs of negatives which are forever voiding each other, cancelling each other's actions and reactions, thus negating each other by never allowing either to exceed its fixed zero of universal stillness.

"The center of my heart in which dwells the universal still light of divine wisdom is the invisible, unconditioned and unmeasurable quality from which visible, changing conditioned and measurable quantities spring to simulate those qualities through two-way wave motion.

"The words you can use for the description of those qualities are love, life, truth, desire, knowledge, power, balance and law. They are the nearest of any description of the true qualities of my heart.

"The true quality of my light is seemingly transformed into quantities by being divided into pairs of oppositely conditioned light pressures of this electric universal world of mine. Those divided pairs are then multiplied into countless octave wave units of light pressures and set in opposite directions, in motion to create the illusion of sequence, change, dimension, conditions and time in a universe where none of these effects of motion exists.

"For example, the sea is an unchanging, unmeasureable quality of oneness, of sameness and stillness. There is no changing it when calm — — nothing to count or measure.

"The moment that quantities of waves spring from that quality of calm, those qualities of waves can be counted or measured. Now there are two points in them which are similarly conditioned. So this creating electric universe is likewise composed of moving light waves which spring from the calm sea of my heart, the still One Light.

"I, the creator, am of one mind. All creation is one whole idea of mind divided into countless ideas of mind divided into countless simulated ideas of mind

29

through motion. The simulation of idea expressed is not the idea it expresses.

"Parts of the one whole idea are only seeming. There are no two separate parts of separable things in the universe. There is but one whole simulation of the one whole self, that is myself — the idea.

"Every part of my worlds move in interdependent unison as the wheels of a watch in unison. The wheels are geared mechanically together, and so the rhythmic waves of this world and all worlds below geared together electrically.

"The whole is myself, and I must keep my body balanced as one.

"Changes of conditions in any one part are simultaneously reflected in every other part, and are sequentially repeated in it, in cycles of waves flowing from my heart to all my universes, galaxies and worlds.

"Now you must go on to higher planes. This spiritual traveler will go with you."

Rebazar Tarzs and I went out of the deep tunnel into the rosy light again where we prepared to go on into the next world above.

CHAPTER 3

The Precious One

riting about a mystical experience is like trying to recite a poem which one has written. Even the nucleus of a poem worthy of its writing is rhythmically formed in a poet's mind during a trance-like suspension of his normal habits of thought by the supra-logical reconciliation of conflicting emotional ideas. A poet learns to induce a trance in self-protection whenever he feels unable to resolve an emotional conflict by simple logic.

This is what I firmly believe to be wrong with those who are seeking mystical experiences. They do have experiences in the depth of themselves but cannot resolve them into words, nor have the communication with the physical senses to give affinity to the objective world. This is what is wrong with the mystical experiences; not that any of us do not have such, but because of a lack of communication we feel that it is not possible, and so many will say, "My experience is greater than yours."

"This is the whole teaching in a minute. We need somebody like Rebazar Tarzs to gather up the experiences and have these inner experiences described openly by each of us. We get the practice of solidifying the thought for description of what was seen, felt and known inwardly. It also gives us a yardstick by which to measure our own experiences. This is not competition but measurement and understanding.

* * *

The Tibetan was silent as we left the city of Kailash and proceeded along the road into another world, which is the upper region of the second plane. He explained that all things throughout the universes were omnipresent, for all things extended through the spiritual traveler himself, and the traveler was omnipresent.

A great light appeared exceeding anything I had witnessed so far in this region. It was more like standing in the midst of a gigantic electric bulb looking outward at the world. We were in some sort of a station, of which there is no description and were shedding the last sheath of materiality of the subtle bodies. Rebazar Tarzs explained that this station was the one where all Souls were stripped of any material bodies before entering the region of Daswan Dwar, the pure plane of Soul. Here we find ourselves clear of all body instruments and behold ourselves as pure spirit.

You will then know all things, rejoice in all things, by direct perception, without the instruments of communication or meditation.

It is hard to understand how one may discard the mind and still know anything. This is because we have been so accustomed to regarding mind as the instrument of knowing. However, it is not the mind that knows, and mind alone is powerless to know, as is a book or any material object. Yet it is an instrument used by Soul to contact objects of knowledge on the material plane.

Rebazar Tarzs explained before leaving the edge of the last plane that Brahm was a selfish God. He

32

tried to get all to worship him regardless and gave little in return, and used Maya, illusion, to keep his followers in control. His use of the mind instrument and the bodies of man are so subtle that we hardly understand the hidden workings of this third plane God.

So we proceeded to the world of Soul, that of pure light and so brilliant that it was like walking out of a dark room into the bright sunlight. It is the world where man becomes Self-Realized. The land of the Paramhansas where they bathe in a lake of nectar. This lake purifies the Soul from imperfections.

All around us was the sound of sweet violins from out of the ether, as Rebazar Tarzs and I traveled over the broad planes, hills and valleys to the Tribeni, a place where three broad streams meet, and into the region of Maha Sunna, where we picked up the secret knowledge of all the worlds below.

This is a region many vast miles in circumference and in the center it is pitch dark. Four sound currents are heard emanating from invisible sources; the jhankar predominates and is undescribable in words. One is entranced by their sweetness and must be pulled away from them by the spiritual traveler with whom he is traveling.

Here are five egg-shaped worlds, full of a variety of creations and each permeated by and governed by a Brahm. Each has its predominating color like green, yellow and white. They are quite vast in comparison with which the entire universe below appears very insignificant.

Rebazar Tarzs said this was the region where Soul gains the highest form of Samadhi called Nirvikalpa. Here one beholds himself as pure spirit after dropping off all material sheathings. This stage is seldom gained by the ordinary yogi. His state of illumination is on a much lower plane and is known to be a material, or negative state; not the real Nirvikalpa at all, but a reflection of the real. All the terms used by the yogis are usually those of many mental states experienced on the planes below Daswan Dwar.

The ruler of this world has several names, Omkar, Parabrahm, Akshar Purush. He dwells in the center of Maha Sunna, the empty realm where all disturbance and agitation of Soul is calmed. This stage is beyond good and evil, beyond morality and relativity. It is also known as the "Tenth Door" beyond the nine doors of the lower creation up to Brahm or AUM.

The king of this mystical world lives in a temple atop a small hill overlooking his worlds. He knows all things and sees all things by direct preception. He can see and gain instant knowledge. He knew we were coming and sent a band of beautiful Paramhansas who met us on the road far from his temple. They led us to our destination.

Every character in every alphabet of all languages in the universe are symbols of what can be found on this plane. One knows and sees all in an instant. Our communication was not with words but by telepathy.

We were without thought, yet we understood. Something that cannot be explained for no words can fully describe what was meant.

The temple was a small, reddish, unimposing building set in a pine grove. It was lighted by the very presence of the Divine One who is forever seated in a chair which looks more like a comfortable couch in a normal, middle class home. I understand that He hardly manifests himself from out of the ethers of this plane, but when he does, he enters into the form which we witnessed; and that the house and form is always there.

We walked up the hill where the sun gleamed brilliantly against the beautiful landscape and flowers, the mighty mountains with their distant snow covered peaks. It made me think this could have been in

India and Tibet, and that it had been especially created for my visit, so my spiritual senses would not be stunned by the very reality of it all. We saw the mighty ruler of this plane seated in his chair, in humble pose, awaiting our visit. If you can imagine a gentle, old man with piercing eyes of indescribable colors, that change constantly, and a short grizzled beard streaked with gray, then you come close to knowing what he looked like.

None of his appearance struck me as much as the vibratory power that flowed out of him. It was astounding, so powerful that neither of us could stand before him. His figure swam before my vision, fading and coming back stronger, until I wondered at the reality of it all. Yet there was the sameness, the likeness of Rebazar Tarzs' firm features, the eyes and the wide mouth.

"Welcome," said a voice from all around us. "Welcome to my kingdom which is another stopping place upon the road to Sat Lok.

"I am known as Omkar, or Parabrahm, but call me what you like. To the Buddhists, I am known as the Precious One!

"So I greet you in this name!

"All omnipresent things are omniscient for I am within them, and within you, for I am omniscient. When your consciousness tells you of my presence within and without you, you will then know all things for I know all things and I am he.

"No form, whatsoever, of my power has being, for I alone have being and that being is in you also.

"Being omnipotent in this kingdom, I give all power to him who asks of Me, but no one may ask of Me who is not aware of Me. See thou to it that all will know that, and manifest thou thyself that principle of power within thine own works.

"I am not this form as you see, but the power of

God which is eternal, always, forever and ever. I live not in this form, but in the power of Souls of all in my kingdom, and below the Second Grand Division none can escape Myself. I alone am the instrument for the God-power, the ever-flowing power of the Sugmad from the greater ones above to the worlds below. I am grateful and humble that it is Me who can have the privilege of being that channel of God. To serve Him in a humble capacity.

"Know this that God is consciousness and consciousness is static, or stillness, whatever you desire to call it. This term is for the power, the divine Soul itself. Words cannot explain.

"Consciousness is the spiritual awareness of Being, of all-knowing, all-power and all-presence. Thinking is the motionless principle in light and sound which creates the illusion of motion, therefore all mind and thought is dropped on this plane. We know and understand.

"The Soul of man belongs to the static, invisible, conscious, unconditioned world of knowing. You express knowing the dynamic, visible, electrically conditioned universe of perception.

"Perception is the electrical awareness of motion simulating the spiritual qualities of God, who creates imaged qualities of separate forms which seem to have material substance.

"Consciousness is real and perception simulates reality through motion of interchanging lights, but the mirage of a city is not the city it reflects. So man is the only unit in creation which has conscious awareness of spirit within him and electrical awareness of dually conditioned light acting upon his physical senses. All other units of creation has electrical awareness only.

"Man alone can be freed from body to enter into God, become God and know God. All other units of creation are limited in their actions to automatic reflexes from sensed memories and recorded knowledge from instinct.

"There is but one power, one God functioning within all creation and that one God is not divided into the more or less.

"All forms in the creating worlds of imaged forms are but electric recordings of God's imagining. They have no existence. Records of ideas are not the idea they record.

"They have no substance. They are but black and white light of sun-centered wave fields of space assembled in vibrating systems to simulate substance in an objective world which is not but seems to be. His power never begins and never ends.

"Inspiration is the language of light which man uses to talk with God, as we are now doing. Inspiration is that deep awareness of the consciousness of being which differentiates the genius from the Being of average intelligence.

"Inspiration in man is accompanied by an intense ecstasy which is characteristic of all who become intensely conscious of their closeness with the Sugmad. Inspiration will cause men to translate God's wisdom into words of man for the Soul of man. They uplift all mankind by re-inspiring all who listen to the ecstatic words and rhythm.

"He who attunes himself to the message of God purifies himself. No impurity can there be in his heart for verily he then is in communion with the Divine Soul.

"All things flow from the light of God and have the light of God flowing through them, even to the least of beings. Though my light of immortal life flows through those mortal symbols of myself it does not touch them in passing. Only when they know the light of Me in them, then they shall be Me and I, then, as the immortal self.

"So ye seek nothing, and by seeking nothing will find Me existing in all. By seeking nothing ye shall find only the static or stillness of God within thy heart.

"All knowledge exists. When man knows the light of this world he knows no limitations, but you must know it for yourself and none can make words for you, of it, for Light knows Light and there need be no words.

"You must abandon your seeking for everything but God. Until you come to this all else is vanity.

"You can know, and understand God alone, by the halting of all seeking, and by leaving behind all the dissecting tools of your mind. The mind is only an instrument given the body in the worlds below the Second Grand Division, in order to give certain outer protection to the Soul and to work with the divine law in acting as the instrument to guide Soul back to its true home.

"In this world all is cause. We know no transient effect. We know cause only, but we can comprehend effect. All divine wisdom is that which exists in cause, and that which is called effect in the creating worlds is only the secondary part of the wisdom of God.

"If the Soul is emptied of all its emptiness then it can become filled with God. The mind itself and its illusions are self-contradictory for the truth of God is beyond human thought. It is beyond all verbal expression.

"Man's realization of his Soul is by no means merely intellectual. It is genuinely a new birth, except that it is hardly achieved suddenly but only as a result of long and patient discipline. Its essence is liberation from attachments to the demands and longings that now hold him captive and the shrinking self that erects a protective wall of separation between itself and all other forms of life. It is these that pose the formidable obstruction that stands in the way of relating the Infinite and Eternal Being that you truly are.

"So you must understand that the Law of Karma is the principle that good choices, earnest efforts, good deeds build character, while bad choices, inertia and bad deeds build bad character. There is always the short way from bad karma to good karma. Jesus showed the way and Rebazar Tarzs, the Godman, can also show the way.

"Life is spirit and spirit is static. Life is not chemistry or germ of matter. Knowledge of light alone will give you knowledge of life, for light is the source of all knowledge, and sound is the spirit, or life itself.

"Soul of man is inborn and indestructible. It has no age, no classification in accordance to earth-measurements and can transcend time, space and causation.

"Here on this plane is where spirituality has its beginning. Here all Holy Ones and all beings are nothing but the power of God, for nothing exists here but the universal body of God in its purest element. What you see that appears to be a brilliant sun, in the strength of twelve suns, is only the reflection of my light, the beautiful music of the sounds of violins coming from the heart of my being.

"Soul is the universal atom of God, and there is no distinction between God and man except that man is attached to forms and so seeks God in the sensory worlds in a sensory way. That is not the true path. And by one's very seeking in this manner he produces the opposite effect of losing God. For this is using God to seek God, and using mind to grasp mind. This defeats all purpose.

"All metaphysical theories are unprofitable and do not tend toward spiritual edification. No particular theory on God can be clearly established as against alternative views. All alike are spun from sense data whose perception, in the cause of each metaphysician, inevitably reflects his variable passions and egotistic demands. Also the assertion of any such theory naturally provokes the assertion of counter theories by others, and this process generates heated and contentious arguments with its accompanying unresolved hostilities and mutual recriminations. It does not promote the humble self-searching and unity of understanding that are essential if the true spiritual goal is to be reached.

"So you must understand that truth that cannot be spoken in love and inward peace is not truth.

"The power is God and the way is God's way, and there is no other power nor any other way. God is that which is the void, having no form nor appearance.

"Divine knowledge is man's power. His thinking is only an expression of that knowledge and the expression of power is not power, therefore the mind and its thinking is not power.

"As man gradually becomes aware of his omniscience, the static of Soul, his thinking of mind intensifies in power in proportion to the increase of awareness of his omniscience.

"Thinking, or the use of mind, is only a wave extension from the center of the divine fountainhead of knowledge which seemingly divides that knowledge into ideas and sets those ideas in motion to create forms of ideas as products of knowledge.

"Divine knowledge is the foundation of man's concepts. Thinking only divides or transfers concepts into products. The quality of man's product depends upon the degree of awareness of his knowledge, and not upon the quality, quantity or intensity of his thinking.

"If you desire to know God you need not study anything whatsoever. You should study only how to avoid seeking for, or clinging to anything. If nothing is sought the mind will remain in its inborn state, and if nothing is clung to, the mind will not go through the process of destruction. What is neither born nor destroyed is God.

"If you wish to understand the real mystery, you need only to put out of your mind attachment to anything whatever. To say that the real God is like the void means that it actually is void and that the void is in fact God Itself. The void and God do not differ from one another, for they are the same; and neither do sentient beings and Godmen, the phenomenal world and the true home or delusions and seekers. They are the same, made out of the same cloth that is God. When all such forms are left behind — That is God.

"Ordinary people look outward, while the seekers of the Way look into their own minds, but the real seeker forgets both the external and internal. The former is easy, but the latter is difficult. Man is afraid to forget his mind, fearing to fall through the void with nothing to which he can cling. He does not know that the void is but the realm of God. This spiritually enlightened nature is without beginning or end, as old as space, neither subject to birth nor destruction, neither existing, nor non-existing, neither defiled nor pure, neither clamorous nor silent, neither old nor young, occupying no space, having neither inside nor outside, size nor form, color nor sound. It cannot be looked for nor sought, comprehended by wisdom or knowledge, explained in words, contacted materially nor reached by meritorious achievements.

"Mind cannot be used to seek something from mind, but the spirit can be used to seek spirit. So any who attempt to seek God through constant methods in which the mind plays a part is doomed to failure. Seeking elsewhere, besides the true way, indulging in various practices and achievements, and relying on graduated progress to attain realization is a false approach. Even after ages of diligent searching they will still be unable to attain God.

"By putting a stop to all analytic thinking, in the certain knowledge that there is nothing which has an absolute existence, nothing on which to lay hold, nothing on which to rely, nothing in which to abide, nothing subjective or objective, then they cross the dark region of this world and come to my temple in the pine grove. Then I will give them the true light and send them upward to the region of the great Lord Sohang.

"It is not by allowing wrong thinking to take place that you will realize God, but at the moment of realization, you will but be realizing He who has always existed in Himself and yourself. Ages of striving will prove to have been so much wasted effort, just as one who seeks a needle in the haystack, and in the end discovers it was in his coat lapel, and just the finding of it was not dependent on his efforts to find it elsewhere.

"This region called Daswan Dwar is the first of the regions of God, the source of all things, which shines on all with the brilliance of the divine perfection, above, and is in all truth, for in it nothing can be apprehended. It is omnipresent, silent, pure, glorious and mysteriously peaceful. Man, himself, must awaken to it, fathom all its depths.

"All that is before you is in its entirety and nothing

whatsoever is lacking. By going through all stages to reach God, man has accomplished nothing, for God is no-thing and yet all could have been attained in a simple, singular flash of recognition. All that went before this in the effort was nothing but unreal actions performed in a dream.

"Somewhere one of your teachers said that the Lamp of Love can be received only by those who have fulfilled the conditions of its reception, and in the same breath repeated that silence speaks a million words, and a million words expresses nothing but silence.

"This is truth within itself for God alone is real truth. And this leads to the further explanation that one must abandon seeking for anything; God itself is realized by the very cessation of all seeking and by dropping of the mind. Now, while dwelling on the earth plane, the Godman will give you only partial insights into these truths, to lead you to the stages where you can achieve the fuller realization.

"Questions are needless for they only lead from riddle to riddle, and like the donkey that loves the hay scattered over the pasture, man goes also from question to question, ever desiring fulfillment of the curiosity in his mind, and never once stopping to look within at the static self, the Soul which is there and realizing it alone can answer all questions on Godhood.

"The cosmic body of God is the only reality in the universes of endless chains. His human bodies are phenomenal and shaped as they are needed in each case. To one who sees things as they really are, all illusions which he had formerly acquired vanish forever, and in that moment he stands upon the towering peak of God's realization and sees the end of his earthly career.

"Above the three worlds Soul can live in solitary

bliss, in union with the cosmic order and with the shapeless. This shapelessness enables Soul to assume any form, and with the very separation from the lower worlds places it within the midst of all this shapelessness. Though you are able to assume any shape, the actual shape is determined by others' expectations. God cannot shape His human bodies as a shadow answers a form, so He appears any way, in any shape. His stature may be minute or enormous, his life long or short, but these are reflections of God produced by the expectations of various beings, and His real body is not there, but it has remained as the static self within the worlds above.

"Yet to say God created the universe and then to say that he stands outside the universe is a contradiction. Neither God nor no-God can exist outside this oneness.

"The whole secret of God is that if you think that the worlds are created by a supreme being, then you must feel that you are powerless to change anything, thus leaving you at the mercy of that creator. You should know that the worlds are of your own production. You may change that world, rebuild it or improve it to suit your own desire.

"This is why there are worlds below, filled with dual substances, for the very purpose to prove to the unmanifested Soul that he is the master of his own fate. And even in this world you have the perfect right to do and to create, although it is seldom done for the pure power and will not have too great an enduring, or lasting substancy, and your efforts are for naught. We do not cast shadows in this region, but let the bright sun take its course in keeping the world as it is.

"If you try to see God through the form of any being, or if you try to hear God through the voice of any being, you will never reach God and will remain forever a stranger to him.

"The struggle within the mind, the conflict of opposite natures is the greatest fault within man. The way is difficult, for man is not subtle enough in nature to grasp the true way to God. Keep silent with your experiences in God-realization, neither think nor analyze them for if you do they will vanish.

"Stop having views and never examine or pursue an argument on God, for others will destroy all that is within you. In time you will be brought to a level of emotional scale which is far beyond that which you formerly reached, and could not hold because of open discussions of it with others.

"Neither discuss the problems of others, even when invited to do so, for in the end, they will curse you and seek destruction of your realization. Thoughts that are fettered turn from truth and sink into the unwise habits of not liking. When you wangle over fine and coarse you are apt to take sides and it is easy to fall into errors.

"The ultimate truth about both extremes is that they are not distinguished. Each contains completely within itself the myraid forms of God's own nature. The Soul is lost by the mind in chaos and never in the void.

"Unless you attain realization for yourself it is useless for philosophers or spiritual teachers to talk about God, the Absolute, the God within you or any other empty name which only serves to lead you astray.

"If a seeker retains the thought of an ego, a being, or a Soul, then he is no longer a seeker, but one who is only hoping. Logic can convince one's reason, but cannot overcome the inertia of dualistic thinking. The intellect may comprehend the oneness of all things, but the thinking will continue to flow in dualism. One must cross the cosmic ocean once and for all to see for one's self the true emptiness of the heavenly worlds.

"As you can see about you when I speak of emptiness it does not signify the opposite of fullness, but rather that unconditioned state in which there is nothing to be given and nothing to be received. Since it cannot be expressed in speech, it can only be hinted at in words, or referred to by use of the word emptiness.

"Some seekers have advanced far enough in their meditation to empty their minds, but once they resume their normal activity they are as unstable as ever. In effect, they continue a condition of mind in which they recognize that there is nothing, but realizing that this in itself is a concrete, self-limiting state quite different from the emptiness of the region of Daswan Dwar.

"True emptiness cannot be included nor excluded. Forget meditation, forget emptiness, forget realization, forget God, forget all, and then you enter into the true realization. Your daily life will become calm and contented, making you less talkative, less worried and less excitable. Then in a glance you recognize your true self.

"Even a delicate movement of your dualist thought will prevent you from entering samadhi. Those who talk too much about realization are struggling, or wandering outside its gates, and will have to struggle before entering into this world. Practice of meditation is not a method for the attainment of realization but it is enlightenment itself.

"Do not attempt to love me, but love God, the formless, who is that which is myself, yourself and all selves. Look only to yourself to give you truth and not depend on any word, book, philosopher or preacher. All philosophers, preachers and sages who have the odor of philosophy, religion and knowledge are not any of these. They are pretenders, those who have pretended to have undergone the profound experiences of God; the faker drawing on experiences of real mystics, and the thieving of turns of speech and materials in hope of conveying a conviction of genuineness. The chief characteristic of these people are that they always state their case with great force and with apparent experience to back them up, and never know why anyone doesn't appreciate their works. They are usually bitter and resentful of others who are in the same field.

"When you realize the truth, you have no delusions concerning your own personal desires nor your self-limited ideas. You know that there is no ego entity existing in yourself and see clearly the voidness of all forms as merely shadow in relation to both subjective and objective elements.

"If one lives in the void, or that which is pure spirit, he can leave all behind and make his own paradise wherever he wishes, in any world where he might establish himself in the spiritual self.

"From the beginning he is God, if you speak of a beginning. As there is no stream apart from water, so there is no God outside you, nor anything within the worlds of God, your fellow being, or anything that is. Although it is always within you, man fails to perceive the truth and search for it. He suffers thirst and does not see the fountain at his feet. Man suffers only because of his own ignorance. The errors of the past no longer exist nor harrass you. You left hell yesterday in your dreams upon the material worlds. Where is paradise? You are standing in the center of it.

"The victory over all, in order to enter into the true worlds forever, can be won, and the key to peace and joy in all lives here and anywhere can be man's by effort.

"This is all I have to say.

"You have listened patiently and wisely.

"Now I bid you to pass through my kingdom into the land of Sohang!"

CHAPTER 4

The Spiritual Fallacy

No matter how you approach the ultimate it must be done by one's own self. No one can tell us how, what and where it can be done. A spiritual traveler like Rebazar Tarzs can guide us and help us over the rugged paths at times, but he will never undertake to lessen the trials of experience. Neither will he add to our load. It is one's own unique way of getting somewhere spiritually which must be done by one's own self and nothing can help.

Most of those who have visited the pure regions of God cannot write about them because of the lack of physical language. So there is nothing available to say what might be found here. Anything one could write would be pallid and sickly beside the actual glories of God's great worlds.

We reached the gates of the land of Sohang, the fourth world known to the spiritual travelers as Bhanwar Gupha. This is the upper part of the mental plane, ruled by the great Sohang, sometimes called Maha Kal. But before starting the discussion on this plane, I want to point out here that few western or eastern religions include the spiritual hierarchy of eastern religions include the spiritual hierarchy; of the five worlds and those nameless regions above them.

I found these regions mentioned only in the writings

of the Persian mystics, the Sufis, some of the Hindu writings, particularly those of the Vedanta Society, and Radha Swami groups.

The fourth plane is well known to many of the ancient greats, e.g., Guru Nanak, Radha Swami, Moulana Rum, Kabir, Hafiz and many others who have been pioneers and left much of their discoveries on record.

When we come to know something about these inner, spiritual planes then it is easy to understand the writings of mystics who speak only in symbols and metaphors because they have not the vocabulary to tell what exists in these cosmic worlds.

Sohang is the ruler here. His name means "What thou art, the same as I." He lives in the upper region of this world, but many of the mystics traveling the path will stop here for inspiration and illumination.

One thing I wish to point out here is that there is a spiritual exercise called Sohang, or Swasa Sohang in which the word "Sohang" is repeated with the inhaling and exhaling of the breath at the heart center, one of the forces of subtle matter within the material creation. It isn't the same as this world, nor does it have a connection of any kind.

The secret of Sohang is that which few know. Yet they look for God everywhere not knowing that Sohang is one of the doors through which to reach the Absolute and must be approached to gain permission and to continue onward to the great ocean of Love and Mercy.

Sohang lives in a city of great, glorious, magnificent light called Arhirit. He is filled with majestic beauty and stately grandeur. When Soul has the privilege of entering the mammoth crystal palace, his home, and see Him, its consciousness is filled with an overwhelming joy and it says to itself, "I am that!" This is the meaning of the word Sohang. At this moment of sublime realization we know that we are of one with the Supreme. In union with the Absolute.

Rebazar Tarzs and I left the plane of Daswan Dwar and climbed the long white road leading through the soft forest and beautiful fields climbing ever upward, really upward through a mountain pass over the Hansni tunnel, which the Tibetan had bypassed for me purposely. The countryside was so beautiful that it was better than traveling through a dark tunnel.

Many pilgrims passed us on the road. They were like the shells of the human form, wavering figures, vaporous and colorless in the brilliant sunlight. They passed without speaking, ghostly eyes peering from beneath monkhoods. Occasionally one would stop to receive a blessing from Rebazar Tarzs.

We came to the entrance of the country which is a tunnel called the Rukmini cavern. One must travel through this strange cavern in order to enter into the fourth world.

Inside this cave is the strangest structure one would wish to see. The road led through a city of gigantic proportions where little men, or forms, if that would be a better description, lived and worked. They were seemingly busy in a thousand ways, preparing what looked like huge bales of seeds, sorting out animals of certain shapes of which I was unfamiliar. Some of these little men ran strange machines that lifted large, heavy boxes onto transportation cars that moved without motors or any apparent means of hauling.

"The city of Uri," said Rebazar Tarzs. "They are putting together many essential parts of the spiritual essence for the worlds below the Second Grand

Division. Those bales are not seeds, but Souls that are unmanifested atoms and need to be sent into the lower worlds for experience. They are gathered up and sorted and put into certain classifications, then sent to the lower planes."

The rest of the way through the tunnel was like walking through a marvelous temple of Egyptian design, with high ceilings covered with strange, weird calligraphy and many pictures in red and white designs that were more than hundreds of feet in height. Then we came upon a pair of ears that were miles high, and beyond them were a pair of eyes, all of which seemed to be made of flesh that quivered and listened and watched us with some strange meaning.

I stepped closer to Rebazar Tarzs, but he nodded and smiled. Then I realized that my seeing and hearing faculties had a million-fold power to understand through them. It was a feeling of peace and satisfaction.

Finally we came out of the tunnel into a light so bright that it hurt the spiritual eyes. A strange feeling of some rhythm started moving around, then I found that we were moving on a spiritual rhythm, on which all Souls here move — it really cannot be explained, but it continued for some time until we passed through the region called Bhanwar Gupha, or Alam-i-Hutal Hut.

We came out on the edge of a high plateau and looked out to see all about us bright islands and many continents which I was told numbered in the hundreds. This was like standing on the roof of a world looking over it, for we could see the palaces on these continents and islands. They appeared to be made of pearls, having roofs covered with rubies and studded with emeralds and diamonds.

"Only the brave can venture this far," said Rebazar Tarzs. "This is why I have often said that only the courageous, the adventurous, daring and enterprising can have God."

He pointed out the black peaks of Bhanwar Gupha mountains gleaming in the distance, stating that we were going to the city of Arhirit, the city of cosmic light, that lay beneath the peak. Strange lights floated over the mountains behind the city, like long ribbons in the sky.

"Those cover the crystal palace of the ruler of this plane," said the Tibetan.

As we moved toward the city, the Sohang Shabda was plainly heard. It was a sound like a keen flute that came from everywhere in the air, filling us with raindrops of nectar. The sun above was of immense light and I found the region most beautiful, beyond description and all existing here on the sound current as nourishment. Those groups of Hansas who were so fortunate to penetrate this region moved along behind us with their followers and devotees hoping that Rebazar Tarzs would assist them in their journey to God.

There are numerous planes and worlds with varieties of creations and inhabited by millions of those wondrous, huge entities of spiritual nature, living on the nectar of Nam. Rebazar Tarzs said, "Kabir reported there were some eighty thousand continents in this region with beautiful residences for those living here."

Most of the color here is of a blue nature. Often the people here, or in the worlds below, feel this is the plane of Truth, and call it "The House of Truth." They claim it is the chief residence of Jesus although I cannot confirm this.

We came to the gate of Arhirit and Rebazar Tarzs knocked, gave the proper words and we entered the city of pure bluish light; so light in hue that we could hardly distinguish the blue, because of the gold mixed with it.

There were rows upon rows of snowy white temples and palaces, on stupendous terraces, flung down from the tall sky, falling into a golden street which bisected the city.

The city shimmered like a mirage upon the desert air, a Camelot of some mythical kingdom. All that was in those childhood stories and fables, or folk-lores of the earth world was coming true. I simply couldn't believe anything was real and now knew where the origin of the fables of King Arthur's stories started. Some ancient writer had a vision of this place and wrote about this city calling it Camelot.

It was a fairyland of enchanted emotions. Sparkling rooftops glistening in a bluish-gold sunlight that was a round disk in a bright sky etched with fleecy white clouds.

This is a cool, blue realm where a shining river of great light runs along each side of the beautiful street, and waterfalls and lakes spread out in various places along the stream. Wild flowers grow everywhere and a geologic wonderland of a city is spread before you.

The highway of gold ran past the high, oriental-style temples and palaces rolling straight into the sky of the Bhanwar Gupha twin peaks, to a glistening crystal palace hanging perilously on a rugged mountain craig. That was our destination.

Rosey-cheeked children rushed into the street, dancing and throwing petals at Rebazar Tarzs' feet. Some hung garlands about his neck. They shouted a welcome to us in happy voices. Then suddenly millions of beings of unsurpassed beauty, blue in coloring instantly materialized and lined the street to silently pay homage to the great Soul who was with me.

We moved onward into the sky, over the beautiful road that seemed to sing under our feet. Reaching the gates of the castle I found it to be completely crystal and studded with jewels of some nature unknown to mankind. The Tibetan said it was a jewel known only in that region. It was called tuani.

The gates opened automatically at our approach. These gates were at least a couple hundred feet high. We entered and trod over a blueswarth which was like newly laid sod.

A door in the palace opened. It was a plain square building lighted brightly by some means which I couldn't tell until ushered into an immense room where was seated the Lord of this Universe whom we know as Sohang, sitting on a dais that was filled with cushions, and under a canopy like an Oriental potentate.

The light from this Soul glistened, shone and radiated in a bluish-white aura so wide that it filled the room and disappeared into the walls. Then I realized that all the light in this region came from this very being. And also, came sounds of a high flute issuing out of the center of the light so sweetly that it draws all like the flute of Pied Piper did the children of Hamburg.

"Come closer," said a sweet, lovely voice pulling at the heart.

I saw a youth with a beardless face, hardly more than twenty-five, dark of skin, sitting on a cushion, inside the light. His face was strangely like that of the Tibetan's with piercing and flashing eyes.

We seated ourselves before this strange youth and listened quietly.

"As Shamus-i-Tabriz said, the image of God is shattered, and He whom we have known as God is dead!

"The concepts that man, as man, has built up

through the centuries around an Almighty Being are now buried and a tombstone has been erected with the epitaph, 'Here lies the body of God!'

"Man conceived God and placed him on a mighty throne, and even gave him duties to impose on the worlds of His nature. From the mansion of Illusion this God punished the enemies of every man, but rained gifts upon every man. Each had his own reward as he wanted it!

"Every religion, cult and philosophy of the three worlds formed principles and attributes which they gave their God. Each disagreed, usually violently, in principle with one another. Mighty wars have been waged with one religion seeking to destroy the other.

"The Christians attempted to kill out the Moslems but failed. Yet more Christians were murdered and slaughtered by one another in the Thirty Year's War of the earth's middle ages than through the whole Crusades against the Moslems.

"What fools have been the men of the dual worlds. Even your Gods have flung thunderbolts at one another until at last Zeus gave away to Jupiter and Thor to Mars, until they all destroyed themselves.

"Man is more concerned with God taking care of his machinery which consists of a brain, heart, bowels and kidneys. As he comes closer to death his prayers are stronger, louder and more pathetic to his God to save him and allow these plumbing works to continue their piddle-patter for the sake of nothing.

"What man has given to the world is nothing, except for his spite for revenge against a society that rejects him. This and nothing more. The spiritual travelers recognize the fallacy that man desires to evolve and only does so begrudgingly because God pushes him into a place where it is best to do so or suffer.

"Spiritual logic? Man has none, but then sometimes his feet comes close to the fires of hell and he develops logic fast in the right way.

"All great Souls are known for their contempt of the world and its pitty-patty games. Count them and name them in religion, literature and every walk of life. If a Soul is not known for his contempt of the world in the dual universes it is because he has lacked the power to express himself in some fashion or another.

"Thus you see all the great philosophies are the outcropping of a traveler's tirade against mankind who rejected him during his spiritual mission on earth. It is not a vengance that causes him to do this but a determination of that restless spiritual one to break the complacency of this bovine attitude of the masses of man.

"The great individual is great because he is aroused, or has been aroused, fortunately, by the spiritual traveler, of the divine latent faculties within him, and not by the fortunes of events.

"The black hole of Calcutta is child's play beside the earth universe into which man wants to let himself sink. The spiritual insurrections are quenched on all sides by the venom of conventional intellectuals.

"So man in his stupidity as the superior being, so he thinks, devoid of the slightest imagination, establishes a God which is a fallacy. What man cannot understand is that pure love and self-sacrifice is the requirement of character, and goodness to others is the only contingent. It is always difficult to find happiness in one's self and impossible to find it anywhere else. Love is like charity, it begins at home.

"The world is naïve and simple and as old and evil as hell; there is a spirit of world-old evil that broods over all, with all the subtle sophistication of man's own invention — Satan. Greed, deliberate greed, crafty, motivated, masked under the guise of world groups for betterment of mankind, yet man murders his saints and hangs his philosophers.

"The disgusting spectacle of thousands of his industrious and accomplished liars engaged in the mutual and systematic pursuit of their professions, salting their editorials and sermons and words with the sweetness and lightness of religious and philosophic platitudes.

"In the world of man beauty breeds only prostitution, but beauty is not always prostituted. Those who do perform their duties to God are grabbed by egoism and attachment. They grow ignorant of Nam and Bhajan.

"It is the habit of the world to persecute the saints and prophets but when they are gone the people weep and repent. Jesus was crucified by His people and Nanak underwent hardships in the Punjab. Those who believe in the saints are led up to the spiritual regions by them. These spiritual travelers will liberate those who believe in them and work according to the instructions laid down by them.

"The knowledge of this world and other worlds in the cosmic universes is a great gift from the Sugmad. Respect it. It is Soul's duty to develop the spark of divinity aroused in it by the spiritual travelers and practice until possible, to experience this realization of Soul every day, with regularity.

"It is impossible to fathom the love of the spiritual traveler for those whom he has taken under his custody. He is more anxious for the advancement of the chela than the chela himself. There is just creative principle for the entire creation of God. All are born of the light of God and the same light shines fourth in all.

"Do not talk of God, but act in God, without conscious knowledge of Him being within you. The macrocosm. The human body is a proto-type of the universe and much more than that. In it are millions of solar systems with their suns, moons and earth revolving in and out. The sweetest of the sweet music is also going on in it, emanating from the true throne of the true King-God.

"This is my world, the land where you are to be — to be God. Know that you are God, Himself. Fall not back on the old powers but live in the essence of God's truth. You see Nam is within me, and it issues forth from my heart. Your heart, the Soul heart is also the seat of God, and from out of it can issue the sound of sweet music. Keep it this way, always.

"Man has been a permanent sort of God throughout the ages. It creates all — the earth, sky, lights and the whole creation. It is all. Soul cannot do without the music of God in itself. This fountainhead or spring of fulfilling nectar of Nam is located in the human body, in the heart.

"Truth, word of Nam is an unchangeable permanence that pervades and sustains the vast creations, or worlds, with innumerable higher regions. It is an imperishable and immortal power — at once the creator, sustainer and the destroyer of the dual worlds. The traveler is that great being who can give you not only the knowledge of that life principle but who can actually link you with the sweet music which is the fountainhead of all love and all light.

"He is the one who has it in his power to grant soul the link with the infinite, while Soul is still in its finite human body.

"In this world you find the smallest thing is largest and the largest thing is small, that being is non-being and non-being is being. With the experience of this visit you may know that all things are possible. You know that one is many and many are one.

"There is no such thing as faith in this world. We have knowledge, and having knowledge is simple, as simple as the child in your earth world who knows that two times two equal four. There is no way but silence to express it properly. This silence is not the past. This silence is not the present. This silence is not the future.

"Realization that you are me has no color, no form, no psychological movement, and no action of dualistic tendency, nor no downward pull. Here in the wink of an eye countless ages, if there are such, have vanished; innumerable names and words of praise have nothing to do with my realization.

"In silence you speak my name loudly, and in speech you manifest its silence. There is no dust upon my mirror, it shines brightly with the light of God. Once you realize that nothing exists, everything being of God is free of being and non-being, you become the enlightened, the perfect One. A Satguru within your own rights.

"I take away your unnecessary burdens but give you nothing in return. Only greater problems for the reason that if you, as all Souls must someday be the spiritual traveler, and must learn to take the responsibility for the greater problems. Yet you find yourself in an atmosphere of peace and this is your power of emancipation.

"If you have realized me, then you have realized truth and hold nothing that is to be realized. If one sees eternity in nimself, he will attain quickly, but if he makes a point in his mind and aims at his destination he will attain slowly. The wise one knows that he himself is the path; the stupid one makes a path beyond himself. He does not know where the path is nor does he know that he himself is the path.

"The traveler, through his all embracing compassion, infuses in Soul his great love and thus gathers Souls at their center behind the two eyebrows. He does this with Souls on every plane in the universe to take them into the higher worlds of reality, light and sound.

"You keep your knowledge of my world intact and not let anything take it from you for this is the golden opportunity to return to the traveler's ways and give service to God. In the lower worlds all philosophies and religions were made for man's salvation but here we live liberated from such claptrap and know that nothing exists but love.

"The human heart is the seat of God in the lower worlds. It has been given man in trust. It must be kept clean for then alone it can reflect His light and make life truly blessed.

"From the word proceeds all things and all things tell of the word. This creative word is called Nam. Truth is one and only one, and men call it by various titles through all ages in the dual worlds.

"Real worship and devotion is purely an internal process unconnected with and independent of any and everything outside the human consciousness. All that is required is purity of self. With this you can worship anywhere under the sky for all that is under the sky is the vast temple of God. There is no place without him.

"The true lovers of God stand out in the worlds like beacon lights to a ship at sea.

"Chant the holy word a million times, yes a hundred million times, and beyond the count until they become such a part of you that the chanting goes on and on into the vast worlds, with them humming in you.

"Here your joy is as high as the vast heavens above, and deep as that which is under your feet. Standing, walking, running, sitting or lying, or whatever you are doing you will always be returning thanks for the great blessedness of having your life come in contact with the spiritual traveler. Be of humbleness always in regarding Him, and be always ready to do his duty when called upon.

"The radiance of my light of truth on this plane surpasses all lights so I am here called the Sohang of Pure Light. Those who are embraced in my light and music are cleansed from all karma and attain emancipation.

"This wonderous light transcends form and description and has the power to enlighten all beings and all creatures that reach my Kingdom on their journey upward.

"Within my kingdom are numberless great Souls who will in turn reach the true home above and take refuge in God, alone, and then will return to the dual worlds to help with the work of the spiritual travelers. The greatest of all enlightenments will be theirs.

"They will earn the right of free joy and opportunity to adore God in His final light. You too will return again someday.

"This is all that I have to say.

"You may pass on into the land of Sat Nam!"

CHAPTER 5

The Secret Teachings

he beautiful sounds begin to sound louder in the ethers and we went on hoping to find the source of it, following the melody like a bee going directly to the heart of a flower for honey.

The road lay bright and long in the brilliant light, like a great transcontinental highway, always moving forward. It reminded me of a long white road in India, centuries ago, during an incarnation.

We went on wondering what would be next, but only Rebazar Tarzs knew. The faint sound of bagpipes reached us, growing stronger as we traveled nearer the border of the fifth region, where dwelled the great Sat Nam, the first manifestation of the Sugmad, the entity known as God.

The sounds fell as pebbles fall from a height. The notes were impassioned, in varying degrees of tone levels. It would stop every few seconds and there was a silence of silences. A silence one could hold in his hand, and a silence that came down like a pressure of a distant storm over the mountains.

I was becoming aware that every moment of eternity and every event or experience plants something in a man's Soul. Just as the wind carries thousands of invisible winged seeds so the stream of God brings with it a spiritual germ of vitality that rests imperceptibly on the love of man. Some seeds are lost and perish but most fall on good Souls and grow.

There is no separation of the cause from the effect. The idea of an apple of the earth is in the pavement of this world's broad highway, and in the light of those heavens, still above us. There are more heavens; how many one doesn't know. The spiritual travelers in their writings mention twelve but there are many more than this.

The reason that some of these planes are not creative in the same sense as the other worlds is that the negative stream of life does not exist in them as it does in the dual worlds. It takes the combination of the negative and positive streams for the creative cycle, and the complete stillness of them, in the lack of motion which gives one the complete static of pure life.

The approach to the fifth region is guarded by a zone of deep, dense darkness that none but a pure traveler can cross. Only he who has the light and power may tread here, and take his disciples with him. This is the start of the Soul into the great worlds of pure spirit where the citizens are pure and in such countless numbers that one cannot estimate them, and there is a joy so great that we in the human consciousness cannot conceive of it.

Since Soul was separated from its home in the fifth region, the Kingdom of Sat Nam, and often known as Sat Lok, it has had no peace nor calm.

Soon as we crossed the boundary into this region a volume of fragrance or wonderful sweetness greeted us at the portal of this vast transcendent realm of concentrated spirituality. This world is never destroyed nor felled, it is the permanent and true home of the Soul, everlasting and eternal. Therefore one's goal should never be below this region for attainment, yet many do have their ideals fixed in the third and fourth planes.

When the Soul reaches this plane it has attained the radiance of sixteen suns. Only then can it behold the Supreme Being — Sat Nam, whose head of hair is so brilliant that one single hair is as bright and lustrous as millions of suns and moons put together.

This majestic Being is the first manifestation of God in the Cosmic worlds.

The light of this plane, which drives away all delusion and darkness, is so tremendously great and dazzling that it leaves all description by words behind. By attuning to the consciousness of this high stage, one goes beyond all dissolution and decay and above all ignorance and imperfection, now and forever to find eternal rest and everlasting beatitude.

The transcendent music of the spiritual bagpipes go on forever and is captivating and elevating. One who hears them is transported to divine illumination of transcendent truth and attains to oneness with the absolute Lord. When you see Sat Nam you cry out, "I am He," or "I am God!" You merge your identity into the Supreme Reality of God.

We stood at the edge of the great darkness of God, ready to test Soul. This is like the river Stix that we looked upon, a dark flowing current that appears to be water. It is spoken of in Greek mythology. While we stood there waiting on what appeared to be the shores of a river in the midnight blackness, an old, old man appeared in a boat and bade us to step into it.

We boarded the little skiff and he pulled us into the deepest part of the gloom. The hand of Rebazar Tarzs was placed upon mine as a sweet, siren song of the water drifted around us. We traveled for a time in this dark world where only the faint sound of the mystical bagpipes could be heard. Finally, we came out of the gloom into the light of a wondrous land where golden palaces were set in open fields of silvery light. The landscape was beyond human description and the beauty of the travelers living there was incomprehensible, the brilliancy of each equal to the light of many suns.

In the distance was a gigantic reservoir like those on the earth plane from which flows the most delicious nectar, out through canals to supply the distant regions.

This world, Sat Lok, which is the world system of the Lord Sat Nam, is rich, prosperous, comfortable, fertile, delightful and crowded with godly Souls. The countryside emitted many fragrant odors and was rich in great variety of flowers, trees and fruits, especially jewel trees which are frequented by flocks of various birds with sweet voices which Sat Nam's great power has created for his world.

This world has various colors, many colors, many hundreds of thousands of colors. They are variously composed of the seven precious things in varying combinations of gold, silver, beryl, crystal, coral, red pearls or emerald. Such jewel trees and clusters of banana trees and rows of palm trees are all made of precious things and grow everywhere in this region. On all sides it is covered by strange golden nets and these nets are covered with lotus flowers made of precious things.

Some of the lotus flowers are huge in proportion, a half mile in circumference, and others up to ten miles. From each jewel lotus issues many rays of light, and at the end of each ray there is a saint whose golden-colored body bears the great marks of a spiritual traveler, and who, in all directions and in countless world systems, demonstrates the love of God for man.

Rivers flow through this gigantic world. There are rivers there from a mile in width to hundreds of miles wide, and the same in depth. All flowing calmly with fragrant waters, and resounding with the delightful music of bagpipes, and once you have drunk of their waters, never again do you have any desire for the worlds below, but clamour with anxiety to reach the higher worlds. You can bathe in their waters and be refreshed with heavenly bliss, furthermore, you can make the waters at the temperature you desire.

All here are gods of the same color, strength, vigor, height, merit and keenness of super-knowledge. They enjoy the same dress, parks, palaces and pointed towers. Their very wish brings whatever they desire; palaces, musical instruments and many things. There are religious retreats here for they all share the God-knowledge together.

We crossed a fortlike park which was pure and glistening in the most delightful light, where terrace upon terrace rose into the sky, and sweet tones of music came from all sides. Children played in the fields while adults wandered here and there in search of wild flowers to make garlands.

Within the center of this park was the throne of the Lord of the Worlds. It was guarded within a small city of light by a gigantic wall with four jeweled crest gates. The watchers at the gates were spiritual travelers with shining, luminous countenance who bowed, with Rebazar Tarzs, in reverence.

The throne of the Lord of the World is within an enclosure of pure golden walls, and he sits upon a huge jeweled lotus, with folded arms; always in meditation. The nearest description I can give is that he looks like an American Indian, in breech cloth, golden-bronzed, shaved head and strongly muscular, a being of at least thirty-five, in appearance. He wears bracelets on his upper arms.

The great light that emanates from him is terrific, blinding, spreading its aura for thousands of miles.

67

His very smile is that blessing which reaches the suffering of the earth world. His body is a shining essence in the sea of spiritual light and sound.

This is definitely the first, limited manifestation of the Sugmad, the Supreme One. He is the power, the light, the great master current flowing down and out into all creation, to create and govern and sustain all regions, like a gigantic stream of water.

This power of audible sound current is the audible life stream which permeates all the systems of the cosmic worlds. This is the positive pole of the spiritual regions.

When you come to face Sat Nam, as I have, you are instantly aware that "I am He!" Love is the holy bonds that hold all the worlds together. Only a spiritual traveler can reach this region and travel into the next worlds above.

Occasionally a devotee from the lower worlds is given this journey through the cosmic regions so that he will know what the life beyond holds for him, and he will become useful for the spiritual brotherhood.

All the spiritual power coming down from the upper regions enter into a perfect manifestation for the first time in Sat Nam, as the first actual manifestation, the complete personification of the Supreme Sugmad. He is the great father of all to worship with complete devotion, if this type of religious fervor is needed. He is so fathomless and impersonal none can approach him even in thought. He sits between the infinite light and the created universes and so in time, when purged of every imperfection, we can approach him as the image of the father and receive his gracious welcome home.

While still in the lower regions and that of the Brahm, the Soul (which is the individual self) is liable to return to earth or any of the planets in the Pinda universe. This is commonly called rebirth and death, the "Wheel of the Eighty-Four." When you reach the pure region of Sat Lok, which is the first plane of the higher worlds, just below Sach Khand, there is no returning to earth except as a spiritual traveler. You become an agent of God and the mission of your escort, the traveler, is over. You are now a free agent. However Soul must travel on, over the most sublime and beautiful part of the journey. For in this region of Sat Lok, the Lord of the Fifth World joins with the spiritual traveler and helps guide Souls to the end of its journey.

First, one must become united with the very essense of Sat Nam in a mystic sense, and so, become one with Him, partaking of all His attributes. Then Soul advances to the remaining regions above, and eventually to the true realm of God.

When the Lord of the Worlds spoke, his voice sounded like roaring thunder. "I greet you both in the name of the Sugmad.

"Come spend time with me and hear my sweet words which will fill you with the wisdom of the secret teachings of God; something which I seldom speak of, having few to listen.

"Beauty is ever occuring within me, and filling the worlds so that everyone can appreciate the light and sound upon which they live. All things are engaged in searching for me, in one form or another, but they fail to see that I live always in their hearts.

"Do you love me? Yes, then always love not me, but the light that is within God and that is God, and that is all, everywhere. I am the powerhouse for God, the first powerhouse in any manifestation of form that you might see. Above this plane your perception of feeling and knowing will be greater, and your power of sight lessened.

"The Ultimate Reality transcends all that can be expressed in words. The beings of all worlds are so many grains of dust in the wide expanse of the universe void, now safe, now lost, or as a bubble of the sea, sprung from nothing and born to be destroyed. But the perfect and independent Soul is not destroyed but remains ever the same; it is identical with me, the substance of God.

"Thus unity alone in the world is boundless in its reality and being boundless is yet one. Though in small things, yet it is great; though in great things, yet it is small. Pervading all things, present in every tiny hair it includes the infinite worlds in its embrace; enthroned in the minutest particle of dust, and yet turning the great wheel of all; opposed to all sensible phenomena; it is one with divine knowledge; it is manifested as the true nature of God.

"What do I speak of?

"I speak of the audible life current. This is the keystone of the arch of God, and the science of all secret teachings. What issues from God is His shabda, His voice, and this is not only emanation from God, but the Sugmad Himself!

"If man speaks in his world he simply sets in motion atmospheric vibrations, but when God speaks, He not only sets in motion etheric vibrations, but He Himself moves in and vibrates all through infinite space. When He speaks everything that is static, as spirit, vibrates and that which is the word can be heard by the inner ear which has been trained to hear it.

"The holy shabda is that divine energy in the process of manifestation. It is, in fact, the only way which the Supreme One can be seen and heard, through light and sound, a mighty, luminous and musical wave, creating and enchanting.

"This teaching is called Eckankar, and is distinguished from all the other teachings of the holy sciences in that it furnishes you with knowledge of

70

both light and sound. It is the very foundation of all systems of science. It is the key to the success in unfolding all spiritual powers and controlling the minds of all. Unless a teacher takes this as a part of his system and practice, he is not a genuine Guru, for Soul can make no development until the human self participates in the training of the audible life stream methods.

"The current of sound from the Godhead contains the total sum of all teaching emanating from God. It is His language to all, and includes all that God has said or done. It is God Himself in expression and it is the method by which God makes Himself known to all His worlds. It is His word and His language.

"When God manifests Himself as myself, Sat Nam, He becomes fully personified, embodied, individualized, for the purpose of bringing into manifestation all the qualities of the deity. So I become the personal creator of all, Lord, God and Father. Here God becomes a fountain out of which the audible life stream proceeds. When you hear it, you hear God, and when you feel it you feel the power of God — the supreme power — or Christ consciousness. Whatever name you desire to call it.

"The Word is like a wave flowing from the river's source, into the universes. It has two aspects; a centrifugal flow and a centripetal flow. It moves outward to the center of all creation, and it flows backward toward that center. Moving upon that current, all power and all life appear to flow outwardly to the end of all universes and back again. Upon it all life appears to be returning to its original source.

"Upon this current, man has to depend for his movement to his original home again, here in Sat Lok. When the Spiritual Traveler makes the connection through the linkup, then man begins his journey home without delay.

"Language cannot tell you what the sound current is, you know and understand it, for it is a language which has never been spoken or written. Yet it has inspired more Souls to higher things of life, including the desire to find God, than all other aspects upon the planes of all worlds.

"Simply stated, this sound current is the Supreme Creator Himself vibrating through all cosmic worlds. It is the wave of spiritual life going forth from the Creator of every living thing in all planes, and by this current, God has created all things and by it He sustains them. In it they all live and move and have their being, and by that same current they ultimately return to their source of being.

"The higher you go in the worlds of God the more enchanting becomes the current of His music for in those worlds it is not mixed with matter and cannot be dulled. The Soul is absorbed in it, and lives in it day and night, and it is his life, his joy and his spiritual food. There is not one cubic millimeter of space in existence which is not filled with this music.

"There is no religion nor philosophy, only the current of God. It is the true philosophy and religion, and still better, it is the giver of genuine philosophy and religion. It is that which binds all things to God, the honey that feeds the Soul. Without it nothing could live for a single moment, nor even exist. All life, including the crawling ant to the tidal wave, the solar cycle, and every manifestation of dynamic energy comes from this stream. From the light of the Milky Way to the flicker of a candlelight in your world, all take their light and power from this grand central power of God.

"That which the physical science call energy, which the Orientals call prana, is only a manifestation of this life stream stepped down to meet the conditions on the material planes. It is omnipresent, omnipotent and omniscient. In it lies all conditions, all energies, latent or dynamic. It only awaits the power of creation to be expressed as dynamic force, in one form or another. It has multitudes of forms of expression, most of which are not yet known to those in the lower worlds.

"All is one force, it is the Supreme One manifested and manifesting. Even the tremendous heat, energy and light of the suns of the worlds are derived from this stream. Every ray of light in the universes is a phenomenon of this infinite stream of light. Upon its power depends the life of every living thing, including the stars in the physical universe. Not even a single rose may bring forth its bud without this power and no child can smile without manifesting it.

"This power has attributes, but I speak to you cautiously of them. Who can comprehend or assign qualities to God? Who can analyze Him? But do you know that from its manifestations, that God, the audible life stream, does have at least three very wonderful attributes? They are Wisdom, Freedom and Charity.

"The greatest of these is Charity. When Jesus said that God is love, he spoke of the life stream of the Word. God is charity and charity is God, so there the riddle is forever solved, but not comprehended for language fails us and the thought is lost in a blaze of light, and that light is the audible life stream, the one self-luminous reality.

"The music of God cannot be heard with the outer ear, but only with the ears of Soul. All have that capacity and require only the development of the inner hearing. It is developed under the guidance of a living Guru, spiritual traveler, and this fact of hearing the sound is a supreme joy for it points directly to man's ultimate spiritual freedom. If you practice the techniques then you will not need to hear only with the inner ears but the outer will also hear that divine joyous sound current.

"Once you find it existing in sound for yourself it will take possession of the Soul of the listener; it recreates him, and he finds himself a citizen of the cosmic worlds. He has become immortal and is beyond all space and time.

"So I tell you that from the sacred moment when you hear this music you are never again lonely, nor alone. In the truest sense you are enjoying the companionship of God. The Supreme One is always present with you, playing for your delight the grandest chorus of all the universes and heavenly worlds.

"There is no other way of reaching spiritual liberation except by Eckankar. Without actual, conscious participation in the sound current, or life stream, no one ever escapes the karma and reincarnations and rides this wave home again. All saints have laid strong emphasis on the Word, sound, but man has neglected it. In fact without Shabda no spiritual traveler could ever manifest on the other planes, and hence the worlds would have continued to sit in darkness through endless ages.

"It is true that this is the gospel of life, the Bani, HU, Word, or Shabda, whatever you want to call it. Whosoever drinks of this current will never thirst again, for within himself is a well of water springing up into life everlasting. This is the water that Jesus offered to the woman at the well of Sychar, and which He said, if she would drink, she would never again thirst.

"Truly, when you begin consciously to participate in this life stream, there is in you a well of water ever springing up, sufficient to supply the whole world. There is a fountain that cleanses you, and then goes on giving life to every Soul who comes in touch with it. It purges the human frame of mind,

Soul and flesh, making them crystal clear. It is the nectar that you find flowing in the rivers of this world.

"He who drinks of this stream of life from God will never again go seeking food for his spirit. He will not look elsewhere for the light, for this is the true light which lighteth every man who comes into the worlds. It is God, the Supreme Father and the wisdom, charity and freedom. This is the great Shabda, the audible life current, which has been known and practiced by the great spiritual travelers for untold ages.

"The Soul of man is reborn, brought to light, out of the dark womb of his own space and time, by the action of the divine spirit, in the form of this life wave. That birth takes place when Soul actually hears the sound just as definitely and distinctly as he can hear the rustle of wind in the tall pines.

"There is no birth without the Word, or Bani, and there is no such thing as contacting the sound until one has first found a spiritual traveler to tune him in with it. So here is the entire matter in a few words.

"Any disciple of a spiritual traveler who has the true experience of the heavenly music, will be like the disciple in the Book of Acts of the Holy Bible, who heard the mighty winds which appeared like tongues of fire around their heads. He becomes filled with light and power and among other things, he is able to understand all languages, including those of the creatures, plants and mineral life, as if he is speaking his own language. This is encountered on the first plane of the cosmic worlds.

"To become filled with the Holy Spirit, is to simply hear and participate in the living life stream, and to become absorbed in it, to become one with it.

"In becoming one with it, you come into possession of the highest power of God's own Self.

"You are to go onward on the path to the next world,

that is called Alakh, presided over by Alakh Purusha.
"Your experiences will be exceedingly great!"

CHAPTER 6

Man and Woman

othing seemed possible except to listen to that part of the world which was sound, a strange melody of bagpipes. Soon everything else was gone, memories of the earth life, the worlds below, all gone and there was nothing; all there was, was only the light sound.

The sound seemed to be something of myself. But then, suddenly, it changed. It was outside, beyond me. It flowed into me from the world beyond, from the light of the city over the land. It came from a great distance, across the cosmic seas and a continent of light, and across the mountains of the world of Sat Lok and the valley, from the deep heart of Alakh Lok.

There was nothing but the sound and light, and beyond them, within them, were the two faint figures of the spiritual traveler, Rebazar Tarzs and Sat Nam, they receded and became one. Presently there was nothing to do but leave for Alakh Lok.

I desired to go into Alakh Lok.

I could not refuse the desire of the strange sound coming from that mysterious region beyond the realm of Sat Lok. It was always a low sound, deep and humming and seemingly a wind, a mighty rushing wind that passed somewhere in the distance, but never touching me.

Strange that at this point a quotation out of the Book of Job came to me. "Have pity upon me. O ye my friends; for the hand of God hath touched me!"

When a Soul finally finds the sound current through his spiritual traveler, he becomes agitated, like a hound after the rabbit, and cannot do without it. The sound becomes his bread and water, and nothing can ever take its place for him. He can do without the light but certainly not without the sound, or Bani.

Now I could understand why the heart beat is based upon the sound current and many of the rhythms of the world: I know why man's mind can be so deeply confused without the sound current. Once he has this, however, there is opened unto him all within his grasp of understanding, the divine knowledge.

We know that ultimate reality is the absolute Soul we strive for in the highest region of God; that nameless world where dwells that wonderous deity whose body is the universal Soul of all things.... and His music is the inspiration for the worlds of the inner cosmic order.

We begin the upward journey passing through the beautiful land of Sat Lok, which, if I hadn't been eager to get on with the journey, would have been a pleasure to stay. This is always the sad part about leaving Sat Lok. For once glimpsing such beauty of God we are hardly happy in any of the worlds below.

We proceeded to where the grand highway came to the border of that vast region called Alakh Lok, where dwells the mighty Lord of that world, we call Alakh Purusha. Rebazar Tarzs said if I had been surprised at what had happened so far that this was going to far surpass all, until my other experiences would be dwarfed in size and magnitude.

The Lord of this world is a mighty being who has much greater powers than Sat Nam, so that it is like putting a child in competition with a man of strength. He said, "Alakh Purusha does not live in the body form as you have seen the other Gods, but more of a round bright form; that is if he manifests at all. It is seldom that he does — even for those traveling upward this way. I have seen Him in many forms but the round, luminous globe of light is the usual form of manifestation.

"One hair of Alakh Purusha's head will exceed in brightness that of a billion suns and moons. That is why He hardly manifests Himself for the very brightness of Himself would burn the naked Soul into cinders of its own atoms. But you will see. Any questions?"

"None," I replied, wondering at the magnificent world through which we were traveling.

Upward and literally upward, was the unknown, the open land, silent and empty. The landscape was mostly a green beauty. Now and then we crossed broad rivers and passed into the hills that were blue and gold in the growing light. It was like walking into the rising sun. It was as if we, not this land, were moving into a great circle, returning to where we had started before. The light became stronger until it had a strange brassy glare that made me cover myself with a hood of mist which the traveler threw up for me.

We were only specks in the vast worlds of God and for some reason I felt that my inner voice was gone and the spiritual hearing dimmed and the sight faded out. Then I remembered that the Lord Sat Nam had said nothing would be needed in the next world; that all would be a matter of perception and understanding through spirit.

I became like a sleep walker and the worlds around us unrolled in a changeless tapestry of dreams. This was reality, yet it was a dream; far more real than that of life on earth.

Then the world of Sat Lok ended, and we stood at the edge of a weird atmosphere, which was a thin light of golden fog, shimmering and dancing.

Rebazar Tarzs smiled gently, "We will be entering this new world now."

We went into the golden fog where the sound was humming softly in the thin layer of mist which was so light it was like rain gently drizzling upon that which was beneath us. Whatever we went over had no description. It was soft, velvety and went under us, light as we were. Within the vaporous light was nothing, no landscape, nor any similarity of landscape. Our motion was a movement, not walking, into the thin golden light. Yet it was a light that had warmth and feeling.

"This is the world of Alakh Lok," said Rebazar Tarzs softly as if not to let his vibrations carry far, and yet he didn't speak with words; the message he gave me was by telepathy. It was more of an impression.

Everything, except for that haunting sound of humming, was silent; a thin tide of consciousness flowing smoothly and unvaryingly from somewhere, within and without me. I was the world and the world was me. Neither was I traveling nor standing still. There was no impression, no perception or time nor space.

The impressions in me moved around among strange bypaths into that which was haunting. In spite of Rebazar Tarzs, I was quivering with a sliding, flowing motion. There was a quality in the dancing mist that was of my own impression, but somewhere in that vast mist of light, something I knew or wish to know had its existence and was communicating itself to me.

Softly, sadly, like a whisper carried down through the arch of light from beyond, there came to me the deepest impression of the ancient, ageless secret of eternity.

It seemed that by some holy chemistry that fantastic perception of sound had transferred itself into electric impulses and was crowding through every fiber of the self. Presently it seemed that every feeling within me was on fire and then again the throbbing sound pulsed through me. Starting as a deep, soft humming, it grew slowly into the monstrous tide of sound and light.

Standing in the mist I felt it nearby, whatever it was, a mammoth ball of light flowing toward us. A warmth and tenderness overwhelmed me. In that instance I knew an ecstasy which I had never known.

There are no words to describe it. It was a thrill, shock, agitation, suffering, inspiration, affection, sensation, pathos, emotion, throbbing, zeal, enthusiasm... a multitude of all emotions. But it was the sound that did it, and the sound entered me. The Shabda of which I speak, only portrays the staggering emotions that are impressed upon Soul at the time that Alakh Lok, Lord of this sixth region of God's cosmic worlds, greets you within His kingdom.

I realized Alakh Lok was speaking in a silent, mute language that flowed into me, within me.... impressing me with the divine knowledge of its own world. Then with Rebazar Tarzs at my side, I waited, devouring the knowledge. It came rapidly without pause and here was what it related.

"You have dared to enter into my Kingdom, yet in the company of this renowned spiritual traveler.

"If you had tried to come alone there would have been a penalty which awaits the actions of such efforts.

"Soul, you are still mortal and must remain in that

81

state until the time comes for thee to be one of us. Yet since you are here I bid thee welcome.

"What is there to be done for thee? There is nothing in this world of mine except the divine wisdom. If you are content to receive wisdom I can give you the knowledge of all things. But you must pay for this knowledge, and if you are agreeable to accept my wisdom, then the will of the Father is done.

"By accepting divine knowledge you will never again be satisfied with your place in the dual kingdom of Jot Niranjan. It is not your place again, but the nectar with which you are being fed belongs to the true son who brings you out of the darkness into light. For one must live in darkness and be satisfied to do so.

"Oh travelers, what is thy will?"

I felt Rebazar Tarzs answering that it was best to impart wisdom as best wished, according to the desires of the Lord Alakh Lok.

Soft laughter pierced me and then a gentle voice impressed itself upon me.

"God made the worlds because of necessity.

"His body existing everywhere was in a sense ignorant of itself and had to know what it could be in divine life. He knew the atoms of His feet were not of the same nature as the atoms of His head, therefore those atoms in the feet had to gain the same wisdom as the atoms of the upper atmosphere.

"In order to educate the atoms of His lower nature, He created the lower worlds of the second grand division, and placed within it the lower negative pole, for the reason of having a place to put His materialized forms. In this world He placed those atoms which did not have the divine wisdom for the very purpose of learning itself, of what its purpose was in life, and to be awakened to itself.

"In the beginning man was simply the atom of the universal body, the Soul itself, roaming about in a darkness of the lower worlds like the fish in the depths of the ocean without any mentor to guide it.

"Then God began to wonder if there was something better to give these poor and unhappy atoms to help them gain the knowledge of their omnipotence, omnipresence and omniscience. He gave them flesh, and by forming this flesh upon the atom, or Soul, He had to lower the vibrations of that world still farther down the scale.

"These were strange beings that roamed the dual worlds in those days, and what you would know as man today would certainly have been frightened had he the opportunity to meet one of those beings in present time.

"God looked over all His creations at that time and found it was not right in the lower worlds, and that man needed something else, and that something else was a mind, which could be used as an instrument for perception, through which to understand and reason out his experiences. Then God gave man an astral body and man was almost complete except for a heart. God reasoned within Himself and wondered if it would be best to give His creation a heart. After eternity, in which God winked His right eye, He decided to give man a heart and man was completed.

"So now He had the atom, which was ignorant, upon earth or in the astral or mind worlds, to gain experience and return to its true home to help God in His work. Within His own Kingdom, the Nameless world, many regions above, He had scores upon scores of unmanifested atoms which were being automatically created out of His own body and lying in stores within His universal body.

"To put them into action, to become experienced and gain God-Realization He sent them down through the worlds below, stopping at the top of the second world of Omkar to gather a mind body, proceeding to the first world for an astral body, and down into the physical world for a physical body, and there it must stay until it has gained realization of its own God-self before the journey can start homeward again.

"God has an affinity for all. None of His creatures are without His affinity, and you may know that through the Shabda, the Word, He gives His life, His love and Wisdom and Freedom to all the worlds, to all on each plane.

"So we arrive at another point in God's creation of His own beings, within the dualistic worlds. That of woman!

"In the beginning man roamed the world without the need of woman, for he was furnished with everything except the chemistry of the feminine nature, and God began to wonder about this. After eternity passed again, God winked his other eye and smiled with happiness, for He had solved the problem of man's lack of physical, but feminine traits which included love, affection and emotional characteristics that are needed for his return to the Nameless world called Anami Lok.

"For a time, if you desire to use the earth expressions, God was puzzled as to how to give these traits to man, and see that he could be fully responsible for himself. God then decided to split the Soul of man and make of him two Souls, although this would make man unhappy until he was with woman, and become a a part of her, and she a part of him.

"So God did this and man had a woman to be the negative side of his nature. There was nothing he could do within his world to complete a task of divine doing until he had the cooperation and help of woman at his side.

"But man rebelled against this principle of God's and tried to demoralize woman by making a slave of her but it did not work; so woman exerted her divine rights and became an equal partner for man. After all, what could man do without her — she became the other side of his nature, to crystallize forms, and to show him a better way to God by using his perceptive side of nature, and not the reasoning faculties. However, on the other hand, neither can woman exist without man. She is dependent upon him for the power of God which flows through him. He has been given a chemical battery which has the ability to draw the power directly to himself, which woman lacks but can take it from man himself.

"This is why man and woman must join to share their gift from God, to others. And for this purpose the marriage bonds were created, so man and woman could under divine law share their own lives and give to one another experiences which could not be gained alone. And to be the balance against one another's nature.

"It is for this purpose that God has created man and woman, and for the great law to keep in balance the apex of divine life in the lower worlds. So if man goes through life with woman, during his incarnations, he must eventually find his Soul mate and be balanced within life, or the universal body of God to eventually become one.

"Now this law of God's enacts upon itself. All things within the body of God must have complete balance. This is the way of balancing man and woman and their natures.

"There is more to this law than just the issues which have been given here. No Soul can enter into the worlds above the plane of Sat Lok without being complete within itself — without having both completed the cycle of balance and entering into the oneness with its own other self, and both gaining the traits of the other.... and in the end, as it is said, becoming the male or the original Soul as God first put on earth. This Soul had the qualities which God wanted, but could not be manifested unless Soul was split into two particular particles, the negative and the positive, for both to develop.

"The Soul will come together again upon the fifth plane, the region of Sat Lok, and there be rejoined before it becomes eligible for entering any of the higher worlds. God puts the Soul back together again, in such a way that it seems that the Soul was always like its original state, and can now return to God to take its place within the orbit of the divine nameless heaven of mercy and love.

"Be not dismayed for all Souls must undergo this process, even the divine messengers as Jesus, Buddha, Mohammed and others. They all were Souls who were in the beginning an atom of ignorance which had to be sent into the worlds for evolving. Eventually they passed through the needle's eye to become Gods themselves, and the messengers of the Absolute Father. You too will become the same, after this journey has ended.

"The traveler at your side underwent the same experiences as you are now doing. Yet you must understand that all Souls will be viewed in God's true world as the high Soul, meaning the male Soul. But this is nothing unusual for if we are one Soul then we are the masculine or male one.

"You must understand that there is nothing of the negative nature in these worlds so that part of a Soul which is negative in chemical nature can never enter these heavens.

"Are you aware that all messengers of God are the male atom? It is true that there are women saints upon the dual planes but they never enter into the true heaven as the feminine Soul — that Soul eventually finds her Soul mate and at some period of life will

86

enter into him, and he into her to become one for God's great plan.

"This law has never been explained to the earth world, although there are teachers who have reasoned it out or obtained it through divine meditation. No traveler actually has taught it openly for certain reasons. God does not desire this knowledge to be given to His creatures.

"He has His reasons, and they being: if it is known openly in the dualistic worlds that such things exist then perhaps man or woman would seize upon this principle for their own use, to grow egotistical of their own worth.

"So God feels that man in his ignorance is better off for divine evolution than if he were given a headful of wisdom which he is going to learn anyway .... someday, and there is never any hurry about pushing him along too fast.

"Man can have his religions and philosophies as toys in the lower worlds for amusing himself. God does not seek to convert man to anything, and certainly does not attempt to change the religions which man has built for himself and now leans upon heavily. If God took them away man would not have a prop.

"God says that whatever religion man has should be a channel for experience and nothing more. It should be able to transform life and until it does, it is a dead religion.

"The way to truth is simple, but difficult, for the way to know God is to know one's self, and to face one's self in one's own consciousness, and to renounce all to let God flood Soul. Then you will become the Soul of the universe, a part of God's body and master of one knowledge which is God, and that knowledge includes all, even God.

"To face truth is to realize that life is *one* in and through its manifold manifestations, and to have this understanding is to forget the limited life in the realization of the unity of life on all planes of God.

"The force of love is that force of love from both man and woman, usually together, and occasionally alone, that can best overcome all difficulties because the law of God is divine love which holds the key to all things. It is possible through divine love for all creations to become God, and when God becomes his creatures it is due to His love for all things.

"Human love is for the many in one, and divine love is for the one in many. Divine love leads to integration and freedom and with its fusion of personal and impersonal aspects is infinite in being and expression. It makes you true to yourself and to others and makes you live truly and freely. It is the solution of all things, and frees, or liberates, the Soul from all bindings, purifies the heart and glorifies the being of all His creatures.

"Even though man and woman will eventually come together again, and be one to enter into the Kingdom of God, they must live in complete freedom within themselves while apart, and be that which is God. Until the final day of reckoning on the plane of Sat Lok, each must seek liberation for themselves alone. For one to seek it and the other not to seek it means that there would be a delay in coming together.

"God can do only what He is allowed to do for His creatures. Even though He exists in them, and they exist in Him the law does not allow Him to act for them — and they have free choice to do what is within their own power to make life greater and grander for themselves.

"Even in the case of man and woman where there is love, where there is oneness, and in complete oneness then God is realized, completely at all times and in every sphere of life, on all planes. The spirit of true love and sacrifice is beyond the conception of truth. This also means to be willing to give to others in suffering and happiness. Love alone knows how to give without necessarily bargaining for returns. There is nothing that love cannot achieve and there is nothing that love cannot sacrifice.

"To those whose hearts are pure and simple, true love comes as a gift through the activating grace of the Godman, and this divine love will perform the supreme miracle of bringing God into the hearts of all His beings. All the same, human love is not to be questioned, even though it is limited. But sooner or later it is bound to break through all limitations and bring the devotee to the feet of God, in the eternal life where truth always abounds.

"Give to God that which you are capable of giving and He will return it a hundredfold. God can and will do whatever man does for Him, and is willing to go a step further with you in loving Him and yourself. What you are really loving is not God, a being on a throne up there in Anami Lok, but your own self, the Soul of your own being.

"To tell you that I love you as God, is merely words, for action must be shown that my love is greater than pretty speeches or impressions upon Soul, and that is the answer that God wants to have for you when you enter into His nameless world.

"He will not require that you love Him as a great Soul, but as one who is yourself, and that you can help in His great cause throughout the universes. That is all He is asking.

"The message of God is greater than any which can be given by Souls which are not within the true orbit of His kingdom. I will let you see further in the next world which is above this one. It is known as the world of Agam Lok.

"It's ruler is Agam Purusha.
"The way has been prepared for you.
"Go to Him now!"

CHAPTER 7

The Hideous God of Life

I used to think my viewpoints and attitudes on life were wrong for the very reason that everybody kept telling me something different. They wanted me to believe their way. Now I have come to see that many things I clung to were right and this experience proved it so.

I was firmly entrenched to my ideals; in a certain knowledge that nobody else knows and that nothing can change my understanding. I had a realization of my own particular knowledge on God, from childhood, and not even college nor all the conventions of society could change it.

The one thing I am certain of is that God is love, and love is God, and all the sweetness and lightness which the cults teach, as well as most philosophies and religions, is not right. Yet on the other hand God is hideous, forbidding, frightening, shocking, pretentious, garish, unprepossessing, ugly, plain, coarse, distorted, unbeautiful, and about any of the adjectives one wants to use in describing that part of Him as power.

However, He is splendor, radiant, resplendent, dazzling, glorious and hundreds of other adjectives used to describe His beauty. How do I explain this?

Did you ever see something beautiful that was hideous? Did you ever see something hideous that was beautiful? Of course you have. Look about you in this physical world; it can be found anywhere, at anytime.

I am now firmly convinced that cults, religions and philosophies are only founded to convince the followers of the invincibility of the founders, e.g., Bergson, Hegel, Darwin, Nietzche, Socrates, Freud, Bacon and dozens of others became the victims of too willing an audience who wanted to glorify them.

The saints and saviors fell into this unstable trap, not of themselves, but often after their earthly mission was over. Most leaders of society and religions can be said to be the instrument of banditry.

One must be the master or slave. History will tell you that. Invent a good principle for your own good, or interpret one of God's principles that can be used for self-advantage and see where it will get you. All of a sudden you are the leader and no matter how rich you might be, some poor, starving Soul believes through self-ego that you need his last earthly coin.

The leader exists only because his followers allow him. He does not have to fleece his flock, but after all they expect a certain amount of it, and if he doesn't, sooner or later they will leave him for somebody who does.

However, on the other hand, if he is too much of a disciplinarian they will leave him anyway. He must strike the happy medium and give neither too much nor too little.

God works in this way. He takes away the little problems and gives you a bigger one and if you refuse it then you are not able to progress on the path. He is building your responsibility to life, for some day you too will become a spiritual traveler, and then you will understand about having the bigger problems. It will be your duty to run the entire universe of all universes.

There is a strange part of me which is deeply creative, and that part doesn't care how it creates as long as it can work with words, or arts and similar things in nature. It is a strange part of myself, that part that always controls me, more or less.

In the past there have been those who tried to quench this spirit or turn it into channels for their own benefit, but I rebelled, regardless of what my senses tried to tell me objectively. This spirit will not be controlled by the conventions of mankind.

Unless I give the spirit its way within me, its own methods of doing, then life gets into hardships, becomes paralyzed and sinks into a mire.

• • •

I felt as if the God of the region of Alakh Lok could be the end of the journey, but Rebazar Tarzs shook his head and we moved onward, actually flowing out through the light, dazzling, golden fog, and upward toward the plane of Agam Lok where we would meet with that strange, misunderstood deity Agam Purusha.

The experience in this weird land where we now were is staggering, stupendous, colossal and all the adjectives one could think of to describe it. But we reached the boundary of Agam Lok where the spiritual traveler stopped and prepared us for entrance into this domain of the seventh world. I couldn't then understand tne wisdom of this, but later did.

This world was covered with a more dazzling, far brighter light than that of the world we had left. It was almost a solid rainfall of bright-whitish atoms falling upon that which we flowed across. Nothing seemed solid at all, and the motion of going forward into the deluge of light was at first a hardship, then I became used to it. The light was finer and more vibrating than any of the other planes we had crossed.

A giant shapeless thing seemed to appear from somewhere out of the light and hovered over us, watching, waiting and staring as if ready to pounce upon us at the very moment it decided. There was an awfulness about it, whatever it was, and about the only impression I had of this shapeless being was that it was like an eagle with outstretched claws. A strange power flowed from it, downward into us.

All I know was that whatever the journey cost, I had to find out what was beyond this golden light which had a strange sound of humming bees, a thousand bees, a million bees, perhaps the whining of a wind, but how was I to know the nature and the actual sound of Shabda in this world!

What can a Soul assume? What else could there be behind all this but God? God was Shabda. I had to find out what was beyond the golden hailstone of light — that trackless waste of light into which only a few Souls had voluntarily entered in the course of eternity.

The sound got into me and throbbed. It was not loud, but low, persistent, prevading and although its presence filled all, it seemed to be coming from very far away. Now it was the sound of moving air; there was no doubt about that. But of something else too; of the slow distant slur of summer thunder, perhaps too, the beating of a deep rhythm on drums; the moving of a vast dark tide across the world of light. It rose, undulated, fell; seeped up out of the rain of light and subsided into it, behind it. Then it was gone, and again it came, then subsided.

I sent an impression to Rebazar Tarzs. "What is that?"

I struggled to get back to something resembling consciousness, but this world was like the rhythmic swaying of a boat upon the sea. Then the first thing I became aware of was that the light had changed into a swirling mass of firey spirals in the distance before

94

us, but nearer and to each side it rose and fell in gentle waves. Huge naked shapes rose out of the misty rainlight like twisted gargoyles. The light had become different, lighter in texture and glittering brightly.

For the first time during the journey into the inner cosmic worlds I could feel the loneliness and life-lessness of a region. It was a pleasing prospect that I felt might confront the traveler in the true God region.

The emptiness of this world had been a blank, with nothing but light; but emptiness of a different nature, ambiguous, suggestive, full of shapes and shadows and the secrets of God.

We passed through the strange formless shapes, and now ahead was an incredulous looking mirage. It seemed real.

What I saw was a tree.

It was a single tree in the golden light, so tall that I could hardly see the top which disappeared into the misty lights, and the roots deep in the light over which we glided. I stared at it.

"The tree of heaven!" Rebazar Tarzs motioned to it.

We stood there looking at it. Suddenly I realized there was no sound. There was only silence, immense and unbroken and within the silence was myself, and a deep listlessness, a torpor that I had never experienced.

So strange was all this that I remembered at this particular moment a verse from the Book of Job. "Canst thou by searching find out God? Canst thou find out God? Canst thou find out the Almighty unto perfection?"

Then came a soft impression from out of some-where. "It is as high as heavens; what canst thou do? Deeper than hell; what canst thou know?"

Something stirred out there in the light. There was nothing but the sound of Shabda. Far out in the light, we heard it humming across the plane of Agam Lok. Looking up there was a sensation of something — the ancient tree of life; beyond the tree was the light; beyond the light were those huge, naked shapeless things, and the region of Anami, the pure ocean of mercy and love.

Those same soft impressions came again in the light, as if a voice was speaking. "What is identity, and what is difference? Why is there eternity and what is non-eternity?"

"I know not the answer," I felt the impression of words running through me like a channel.

"Fool!" The impressions thundered within. "Why did you come here after gaining the wisdom of God on the planes below?"

The electrical impulses ran out of me into the light. "I come because the test was passed and I want God!"

The voice intoned. "You want God! What is God, you earth worm? You sniveling, pallid thing!"

"God is light and sound!" I flashed back.

A bellowing laughter roared through the light, yet it was not a sound but an electric movement, a power that ripped and tore into me, a motivating motion of light sensation. It thrust into me, with a clash, collision, shock and an impact that was astounding for I had expected this God to be gentle, more than Alakh, more delicate in nature. But this was a mistake and soon I was to see that he would tear off every veil before revealing the true Godhead.

Something came out of the light, a shapeless thing like a cloud, smothering me with its flowing motion. It attacked me with an impelling force of dynamic onset. It slashed, slit, split, ripped, cleaved, wrenched and dismembered me with its terrible forces.

"Power! Power!" It shot atoms of sound toward me. "Power! That is God! Understand that, you fool!"

96

"Nothing is greater than power. With power you can do anything. Defeat any enemy, construct the good, and be the greatest of all things!

"The fool who knows that his weakness is his enemy is wise. But the fool who thinks his weakness is his strength is a fool indeed!

"If you do not understand power then it is your own undoing and not the fault of God, for God is power and power is God. Understand that and you will know the true secret of God.

"Since I am the universal body of God, then I am the power of God, everywhere at all times. There is nothing without me, and nothing can have being without me. I am even greater than wisdom and greater than all the attributes of God. Not even love is as great as I!

"If you let me enter into thy heart and stay there I will give you all; including every characteristic and trait needed to take you into the higher kingdom and remain there.

"The essence of spiritual realization, in relation to the blindly craving and frustrated unhappiness for power, can bring liberation if rightly understood. Its dependency is peace and bliss but its product is power. By power I mean no dependence of attachment to anything or object through which one might hope to find his longings fulfilled outside this great power of the universal *I*. It is an unlimited self-giving quality that gets power in return. Moreover, it is a condition of growth toward such an experience that one expresses at each stage as much of his power ideal as his spiritual progress permits.

"I preach the true doctrine, the true Ananda, that means that no teacher should give all to the world, only that which man can take, and then it should be only in the quality of power. Give to me, and in return

I can give you what you need in life, the control of my universal body."

I spoke out against this, with an impulse. "Why should I want power? Love is greater!"

The wave shot back, in staggering power. "Love!" It impressed upon me in a silent, powerful force. "Love? What is love? Only a small, half-developed quality of God which has not the power to push itself out of the regions above into the lower worlds.

"Look for yourself. Is not hatred more powerful than love? Can't you do more for yourself if you have revenge in doing it? This is only a form of power, a channel of divine power which can do anything and since that is a part of myself, the Soul of Agam Lok, then you can take and use me for greatness!

"As it is now you are the trained seal of the universal worlds. Love rules your life. If you are put in one corner while the teacher shops you will stay there until he returns.

"You too can be the Master and have followers who will come and worship at your feet, and then can carry the torch for them to see the way. Your life can be your own, or it can be someone else's, and always at the beck and call of another. God gave you free will to do your own choosing and this will be for you to do. Nobody else can do it for you.

"You have the freedom to be and the freedom not to be. The path of power is the true way and through this you can overcome craving and obstructions which block the path to spiritual realization. Not only in achieving your own perfection but for the sake of a deeper oneness with others and for the greater power to serve them. Even those who are your enemies. By the realization of the divine power you will come to know this.

"Let each man direct himself to what is proper wherein the power is concerned; then he can teach others, and no one will suffer.

"Too much of the power for those in the lower worlds, knowing not how to handle it, and they will be literally burned alive in their material bodies, for nothing is greater than the power of my Shabda.

"If you have the divine power aroused in you then you can accept any responsibility regardless of how huge, and whereby if it is the Lord of the Universe, then you can easily adjust all problems and obstacles within these worlds.

"The Lotus of the Firey Light gives you a greater understanding of the power of the Absolute Father than any of the ways of gaining insight into this divine aspect.

"The Lotus of the Firey Light is that set of laws which have been derived in this world for any seeker of God to have understanding of the greater Soul before going into the Anami Lok. They are:

"First, The only real power is the power that God is the inner power in all things, and divides itself on the lower plane into negative and positive elements.

"Second, The only real control of this power is through the absolute knowledge of it, and the ability to let the God element within you have charge of it at all times.

"Third, The only surrender to this power is that in which the Soul becomes so much of it that nothing can distinguish the Soul from it.

"Fourth, The only real existence of the power is that understanding of the one and only God. He is the self in every self, and that God is myself, the Lord of Agam Lok. For I am the universal body of God.

"Fifth, The only real love is to have love for that power which is within the self, and then you can encompass the Light and the Sound.

"Sixth, The Sound current or the Shabda is that part

within you which is the power that you are always seeking. Look for it and nothing else.

"Seventh, The love of Shabda, or Bani, develops the Firey Lotus, the color of deep golden red within the heart, and this opens the heart for more power which is the Light and Sound.

"Eighth, If there is hatred in the lower worlds, for any of God's creatures, turn your faculty of inner vision (the spiritual eye) upon the Lotus of the Firey Light, and see it there. Then your hatred will change to nonattachment for the good in man.

"Ninth, All passion except that for good can perish in the Lotus of the Firey Light, and if you desire more than that, keep the spiritual eye always open to this light.

"Tenth, I am that Lotus of the Firey Light. I am the golden light which you see around us, and that which is never manifested because God does not want His subordinates and coworkers in the lower forms. So I stay the formless and the silent.

"You can come to me whenever you desire. Look for me in the eyes of the spiritual travelers, and let your eyes see me in the mirror when you look into it. There I am always, the silent, the ever pulsating and the eternal power which is God and the aspect of God. So I am God, and yet, more than that, I am also you.

"Life is never anymore than what it is now. This is because life is simple and so is the state of all things within the body of God, and this includes God, Itself.

"I am the Hideous one. My face is so terrifying that God does not let anyone see it. It is a masker's mummy, and that which if looked upon would paralyze those who see it. The occasion has been in the past for some to have gazed upon my face and in doing so reported to the lower worlds that God is awful, terrifying and fearful. That is not true, for when you meet with God, there will be a great understanding, a great peace and knowledge of something you have never fathomed.

"My countenance is ugly because I am the custodian of the power; that mighty divine power of the Almighty Father, and it is so great, so untamed that it takes my strength to keep it in line. It is ten billion times stronger than anything you might think of with strength and often that many times over.

"The power can give. It can give you the virtues of Godhood, if that is what you seek. Certainly it will keep you in strength and courage for facing the Lord, and maintaining equal balance in the greater worlds, those which are below and which mankind does not want to leave.

"The spiritual traveler is one who, having attained the goal of purification and emancipation, refuses to stay in the world of Anami Lok, out of devoted love for mankind, to remain in the dual worlds to help man out because of consuming zeal for his devotion and loyalty to all. He asks God to postpone his own entrance into perfect bliss because his sense of spiritual oneness with others leads him to prefer to work with them, and lovingly serve the race of men until he can find enough to take back to their true home again.

"No longer do you need your faculties for perceiving but those which the deeper inner ones, the Soul consciousness, brings the instinctive side of man into his true self again.

"So you are now the blind, the deaf and dumb, led as the lamb is led by the shepherd.

"You do not look upon feelings as yourself, think not that yourself consists of feelings.

"Do not look upon perception as the self.

"Do not look upon the atoms of the Soul as the self.

"Do not look upon consciousness as the self, thinking that the self consists of consciousness, nor that consciousness is the self, not that the self is in the consciousness and that you are possessed by anything in this state, that would be that you are consciousness, and that consciousness is yours.

"Then what are you? Do you not know? The answer is so simple that I cannot grade you for it for you are nothing more than a single cell in the body of God — in the universal body.

"Be not dismayed at this discussion with you, my exalted one. After all it is my duty to see that you are well fitted to enter into the kingdom of God; and this is always my pleasure to beset the seeker on all sides, and you are no different from the ones who have reached this plane and became fearful of what was happening to them.

"He who is beset with fears has no need of God in his heart. In the beginning let me say that God has no need of anyone who has fear. Truth is all there is and since it is all, then perhaps we can show you that the only way to have truth is to show you the way to have power.

"The way to have power is simple indeed, it comes through quiet repose. The more you become still in body and self, the more power you will generate. It is not a real stillness but an active, quiet way not seen on the surface by the senses, but inwardly. I am employing the metaphor for the use of this.

"If you were to cross the river, would you go about building a huge bridge with your little hammer and nails, and saw? Of course not. You would first employ meditation upon how to get across the river, and the minute you sink down inside the real self, then somehow the latent energies are released and you then would be with God, and being with God always finds a way of contacting some part of its other cells in the body.

"Perhaps it would be a boatman who would come to your rescue, and this is the simplest form of power which can be demonstrated. In a sense this is also related to ultimate reality or salvation. If you send out a call to God for salvation then it is a true request and God will always answer. For you have never actually sent a message anywhere since you and all living things are a part of the whole. You only ask another part of yourself, the universal self, to fulfill your request.

"The power is within you, and the way is within you. You are not really anywhere outside yourself, but inside. Neither am I anywhere except inside myself. We are the worlds within worlds, and within the universal world. How can you conceive this? Only by realization that it is the power that brings you to God.

"By clearing the channel you come to this realization that it is you, and then into the realization that it is God. One cannot go higher than this. This is the reason that one needs power to advance on the path. He cannot do without it. Yet on the other hand if he should abuse the power of God, then he will be delayed in realization of God.

"Since you are God, nothing could be more fitting than to meet yourself.

"You may advance into the world of Anami Lok, the true home of God.

"May the blessings always go with you!"

CHAPTER 8

The Spiritual Malignancy

The road to God is long and every inch of the way has to be won against resistance. No quality is needed more by the seeker than patience and single minded perseverance with faith that remains firm through all difficulties, delays and apparent failures. Somebody wrote something like this long ago, but their name fails me now. But it is certainly true for we hesitate even before the spiritual traveler and when the time comes for departure from the body into the other worlds, resistance is so strong that it will not let us leave the body.

I have no description for that God spirit which enters one and lifts us up like a feather floating on a stream of wind. All the old doubts left me as we moved along; in their place was a quiet confidence, something which was unexplainable. One must experience it to understand. All the seeds that God had previously planted had blossomed into a tremendous harvest.

It is God's love that warms me in the sunlight and His love that gives me the cold rain. He feeds me my bread, brings the chilly winter days and hot summers, the light winds to cool the body, and the seas with its thunderous surf, the whistle of birds, barking of dogs and clamoring of children along the streets. To be a part of them is my great fortune and to revel in His glory for they are all in His universal body; part of the audible life current with its great music that sings to any who listen.

All the worlds of God are of countless parts and are wired together by an electric set of nerves which are the part of the divine power that we call the ECK-Power, or Christ Consciousness or love, and which informs each part of the universes of the ever changing condition of every other part. Especially is this true of the lower worlds where creation is a constant part of its nature.

Man always has an instinctive communication with God. If it were not so man could not survive or develop. Instinct is a mechanical faculty and also a natural one. It causes the mechanical actions to take place in the body to meet the necessities of existence. It certainly has greater use in the animal world than in man's world.

Although man has reason, imagination, creativeness, inventiveness; instinct in him is greater. The explanation for this being that the faculty of instinct is therefore God's control over the actions of his creations. Man's involuntary actions do not know their purpose but God centers and controls every atom of His creation and each must fulfill its destiny.

The conscious mind does not sleep. Sleep is merely the negative half of a wave cycle of electrical awareness of God, and awakefulness is the positive half. This is the explanation why the true God seeker sleeps but little — it is a waste of time.

So this brings us to another point in the advancement on the path to God. Conscious awareness is knowing. Unawareness means that we do not know yet. Since knowledge is within you there is always the way of knowing what is needed to know at the time desired.

When one reaches the upper worlds he finds them to be the conscious planes of knowing. Since the senses take no part in these regions, all is at the instant demand of the seeker. The senses, however, are electric pulsations and belong to the thought world of motion and do not respond to the stillness of the upper worlds. As motion itself is non-existent, also are the senses non-existent.

Underlying all in the great worlds of God is the law of balance. All is completely in balance in God's universal body. This is the great principle that man completely overlooks, and if the scientists of our day would look first for this they would find the easier way to unravel the mysteries of the physical universes.

Balance is the principle of unity, of oneness. It is the stability which lies in the Godhead. Balance is the foundation of all the planes within the cosmic regions. Within the three worlds this law is different; it works in different ways. There is a rhythmic balanced interchange in all transactions in nature. Here the balanced interchange simulates oneness by interchange between pairs of opposites. Effect is always seeking to find stability through instability but never does, but always balances through stability.

• • •

Excitement began to grow greater for we were getting closer to the last leg of the journey. It was like the excitement of a child only a million times more joyful.

Then another thing happened.

It was something I had no idea would happen but then my awareness of it was abrupt. The Lord Agam Purusha came in, suddenly seized me with sharp talons and pushed, pulled and worked in a massaging manner that was astounding but painful. The sound whistled through me and the hideous laughter rung around me and was like a nauseating pulse of electricity.

I was tossed like a ball in the air, and finally came down on a soft flooring of something that caught me, uprighted me again, and there I stood with the strangest thing going on around me. The whole world of light had disappeared and Rebazar Tarzs and I were standing on the edge of a terrible gulf looking into the depth of the softest light you can ever imagine.

All was emptiness except for that light, transfixed and frozen in what appeared to be a landscape of softness outlined like a quivering light, and atoms of light dancing before our eyes. Except for the most gentle and barely audible tone of music... sweet music that made me wild to find the source... then there was an immense and absolute silence.

The softness of the landscape, of the endless sweep of rolling hills, of unimaginable loveliness, no longer a part of the world of intense burning firey light, but instead the sweetest, the most beautiful light.

As I stood watching, something of a new confidence entered me. The fears of Agam Lok left me. I was shorn of all torpor. Like the world I stood in, everything was stripped clean and naked; the light of Agam Lok had scoured it, the God Agam Purusha burnt it clean, perceiving clear beyond the journey to the journey's end, beyond any illusion whatsoever to reality.

Here was the end of all things, the home of the Sugmad, God, the fountainhead; the bones, skull, carcasses of all eternity that stood in the center of all light. Here too, I was laid bare, revealed, beyond hope, beyond fear, beyond all, in emptiness, meaningless, and nothingness. Here was the world to which all worlds flow, the waste in which all things had their beginning and to which all things returned. This was the end. The answer. Truth! The Sugmad!

Then I saw it. You might say it was a mirage, an hallucination, the trick of this world. But then I did see it. The light of God! It was standing above all in the center of the world; the light was fuzzy, shiny and bright, not too bright, just enough. It hung in the center of the landscape within the empty space of this world, that great mass of light, so immense that I cannot describe it, gleaming in the gulf of space. While watching it I began to pray, not in words but in impressions.

The scene passed and I felt myself moving gradually, a motion of going into something, a flowing like water. That is the closest description I can give. In a sense I was the same fluid as an atom of spirit. Yet it was motionless, with an impression of watching, feeling the flow and the deep motion in every fiber of myself.

The impulse went through me that the journey had ended. This was living in God. The music was keened, high and thin, as if coming from myself. There was no seeing, no hearing, no feeling, just knowing that I was a part of the Absolute — just the intelligence that has power and freedom.

Freedom! Yes, that was it. I never had freedom before. This was wonderful; the freedom to move as desired anywhere at any time. Then I knew that it wasn't the music that had been heard but a suspension above me like an almost palpable thing; it faded, spiralled upward and became a part of the sound. Again it was there. It was the softest sound of breathing.

I waited.

"Who is there?" I sent out a vibratory command.

The wave hung in the ether. It moved out and came

back like a bolt from space, but I shook it off and waited.

The light became very strong around me, and I knew that I was standing in the center of it, suspended in space, an atom within the light atoms; there was no distinguishing them. Nothing! That is all I can say! Nothing!

I was a part of that cloud of light, a flaming robe around me, in the center of this blinding light. Something entered into my heart, and there was flaming bliss, a glorious light that was the devotion, the adoration, aspiration, reverence, the glory of God, and the divine grace which all writers speak about when becoming one with God.

I stood in the center of a mighty, gigantic light, with the current throbbing and pulsing through me.

This was the King of Kings! Lord God! The Lord of Lords! The Almighty! The Absolute! The Supreme Being, the author of all things! The Supreme Creator; The Infinite. The Eternal! The all-powerful! The Omnipotent. The all-wise and the all-merciful. The all-knowing, The Omniscient!

This was the Holy Self, the spirit of truth, the dove, the comforter, and the Spirit of God, the Sugmad.

Then I was God!

"Preserve, uphold, keep, perpetuate and immortalize this moment, my son," said a low, rhythmical voice within me.

"Ye are blessed, sanctified, hallowed, absolved and glorified!"

The voice ceased and out of the depth of myself it began to speak, within the same round tones as of my own nature.

"I am the divine, the heavenly Soul, the celestial being; hallowed, sacred and sacrosanct.

"In my name am I!

"In myself am I!

"In my body am I!

"In all am I!

"I am the Deity!

"I am the Divinity!

"I am the Godhead!

"I am the Omnipotence!

"I am the Providence!

"And I am the trinity, the holy trinity, the trinity in unity, triunity. The threefold unity!

"I am God, the Father, the maker, the creator, the preserver. I create, preserve, head the divine government, and the hierarchy!

"I am God the Son, Jesus Christ, the Messiah, the Anointed, the savior, the redeemer, the mediator, the lamb of God, the Son of Man, the good shepherd, the way, the door, the truth, the life, the bread of life, the light of the world, the vine and the true vine, the King of Glory, the Prince of Peace and the Spiritual Traveler.

"I bring salvation to all Souls, redemption to those who want it. Atonement for the suffering, mediation, intercession and judgement.

"In creation I create, mold, form, fashion, manifest.

"In preservation, I uphold, keep, perpetuate, immortalize.

"In atonement I redeem, save, expiate, intercede, mediate.

"I give inspiration, regeneration, sanctification, consolation and grace.

"I have many names by all people. The essences of the Universe, Radha Swami; The Blessed One; Zarana-Akerana, the Infinite Being; Ahuramazda, or Ormad, the Lord of Wisdom; the King of Light; Allah, Buddha, the Sugmad and many others.

"Whoever wants me can have me!

"But many deny me through spiritual malignancy!

"This is the only way I can be denied — and that terrible illness is this.

"Rebelling against my name in complaints and disharmony.

"This will stop the spiritual growth and keep Soul out of its true home!

"Be virtuous, have self-control, self-denial, and enter into my works whole-heartedly. These are the qualities that make you matchless, peerless, saintly, saintlike, angelic and godlike, and brings you to my feet and makes you a spiritual traveler!

"You are the traveler now! Look into your heart and see! Are you not he, and he is you.

"Who can tell you the way to heaven? Can the clergyman, the doctrine of any religion?

"No, only the Bani, the sound of the heavens!

"Only the spiritual traveler, the Godman!

"Only you, Soul!

"Listen to none, but these three! The trinity of yourself!

"You have now realized God!!

"You have now entered into the Kingdom of God; Heaven; the heavenly kingdom; the heaven of heavens; Paradise; Eden; the Holy City; God's Throne; the City Celestial, the Abode of the Blessed!

"Dwell in my bliss!

"This is the ocean of love and mercy!

"I am not a being, a Soul, nor a thing. I am God, the unique! That is all the description necessary!

"Who are you?

"You are also God! You are myself! I!

"My first principle is that this true cosmic IS!

"My second principle is that there is no God but me, 'I,' not me as you know, but that which is within you, the Self. Therefore all is God, including the lowest of life.

"My third principle is that to have divinity then you must dwell in the center of my light and sound; and since light is God, and God is light then it is everywhere, and has no focal except in each Soul. Thus I must dwell in the light within Me!

"My fourth principle is that no truth is greater than the lie, and truth is never greater than no truth for the latter is the shining ideal which God holds before the Soul in his true kingdom!

"You must live for me, but not die for me!

"To die for me means separation. There is no need of separation from me!

"To love me most is to understand and feel the need never to harm or hurt any of my beings anywhere in the worlds of my body.

"To love me greatly then love your fellow Souls.

"To harm yourself is to complain against the treatment of your fellow beings. And this is ceasing your love of me!

"I love you dearly when you are just God!

"Be guided by love and truth. This is the only way into the heart of the great Soul. By loyalty to the unchangeable truth you can hope to be established in abiding peace.

"When I speak, my word manifests somewhere in the world of worlds as truth!

"My word can never be comprehended by mind. It must be taken in by the heart and arouse you to desire me.

"My love and blessings are ever with you. Take care of them!

"The manifestation of truth is my word!

"With the dawn of realization of the unity of life, hatred and dissension within your heart comes to an end!

"Unfaltering love and unfailing understanding unites

you with all Souls within all planes of the cosmic worlds.

"All brotherhood of men is based on the realization of oneness of myself.

"Spiritual liberation comes from the practice of Shabda!

"Man, when properly trained, is able to detach himself from the physical body while living in the body and travel to all parts of his outlying universe.

"Man does not know the actual worlds, or kingdoms inside himself.

"I have loved you more than you have loved your defilements.

"The supreme test of discipleship is to have love for all that lives.

"The root of all that is evil is within yourself. Not within others.

"To give and give only, never once thinking of rewards, is the beginning of immortality.

"No man can become God by fleeing from pain, or seeking comforts, pleasures or by attachments with worldly people.

"Serene detachment is the last step in the separation of Soul from worldly bondage.

"Man shall not glory in his own enlightenment while he looks down upon others struggling in pain and ignorance, holding himself upon a pinnacle of self-righteousness, or vain glory.

"Soul of man is the experiencer of life.

"Man is the wonder of wonders, but he knows it not. If by the grace of the spiritual traveler your spiritual eye is opened you realize that the true temple of God is the human body.

"For true realization you must look within because there you have my indwelling spirit. In the Self are all things.

"All transcendent secrets, all heavenly treasures, all divine blessings, all knowledge, all bliss, all love, all things are within the Self.

"If you live in these transcendent realms beyond illusion, you will someday become the Lord and Master of the whole universe.

"To become one with God, one must be brave and active. But activity is not confined to the lower worlds, but chiefly in the higher realms.

"The mystics of Bani, or Word, move in the higher planes of absolute consciousness. They are in the lower world but not of it, and want to take others into their high stage of spiritual bliss and knowledge.

"Salvation is here and now!

"Unless you find God now and reach the subtle spiritual stages in this life time, where is the guarantee that you will do so after death?

"You should not rest on getting salvation after death. You can find the transcendent secrets and know the ultimate reality in this very life, before your physical death.

"True life cannot be had unless, during your earthly life, you crossed the borders of death and, so to speak, was born again on this spiritual plane.

"Shabda shows you how to die before actual death and it releases you from the bondage of karma and maya.

"The infinite is contained in the apparent finite; the eternal resides in the outwardly evanescent; the transcendent Absolute, myself, is screened in flesh and blood; I, the Supreme Being, am concealed in the human body!

"Whosoever seeks me elsewhere, other than the human body, and in the bodies of others is a fool!

"The real living entity is the Soul. It is Soul that puts life into the body. All things, body, mind and Soul are closely tied by strong desires and bound hard by chains of egoism and delusion. This is the knot of conscious and the unconscious ties. Soul is conscious, all else in man is in its unconscious state. It is the Soul that lends both consciousness and power.

"Mind is the essence of the Word, while Soul is the essence of myself, the true deity.

"My word is the transcendent and all-prevading form of God, it is my heart and Soul, my essence and existence. My life and light; it is my very own being, my very Self, but it manifests itself in the form of divine music, unending and eternal which is known as Bani, or the sound current.

"The sun that never sets is visible only to the naked Soul, and my music is audible to the spiritual ears only.

"My will is one with the word, the infinite and eternal word, which is without beginning and without end; all prevading, transcending all distinctions and limitations, ultimate and absolute, one with existence and life, the final reality of all realities. It is not bound by anything. It is all in all, boundless, infinite and ever-lasting.

"There is no writing of the word. It envelopes all space and permeates all life; it reverberates through the range of infinite time, from eternity to eternity.

"But in the worlds of worlds there are millions of names for me but none brings you salvation. My original name is a secret repetition, that very few indeed know.

"By the singing of 'Sugmad' you can gain salvation. This is the original, genuine, eternal name of myself which is a secret and transcendental repetition.

"It is my essence and being, my unwritten law and unspoken language.

"Egoism is a deep disease but Shabda can take it away from you.

116

"The singing of hymns will not remove egoism and vanity, the only antidote for it is the transcendental Shabda.

"The name of myself is the Sugmad — the all in all. It is the true light name of myself; it is the reality of all; it is the staff of all existence, the light of all knowledge and the repository of all truth.

"My eternal voice is the genuine nectar that drops from this most high plane. It is the true Bani that resounds in all space and through all time. It is the true devotion that sings eternal praise of my Absolute Self.

"It is the ocean of bliss and love, the highest, purest and most transcendental. It is the ultimate reality, the absolute supreme being, transcendental, infinite, eternal; it is all in all.

"My voice is the support of the whole fabric of creation; it is the creator and sustainer of all worlds and universes.

"Within all beings, and within all things, is my eternal word which brings the cosmos into being, which creates the many universes, and gives shape to all things.

"All religions state that my word is the creator of universes. My word, my light does shine among all peoples, and lights every man that walks in the world of duality. My word is real life and true light. Ordinary light shows only phenomena, only what seems, but the light of my word reveals to you what is the reality behind all appearance. All mystics have recorded their spiritual experiences of it.

"Of whatever creed, race and caste, all mystics who come into the higher spheres within themselves mention this word; this Shabda and this light in their writings left for the records of man.

"In your world, O man, the true light is for you,

and this true light is Shabda without which you would remain ignorant.

"For your own being there is no other way of liberation save for my divine melody that draws it up above all matter into the realms of pure spiritual and transcendental planes.

"The true nectar is Shabda!

"The word brings you to the eternal life of the spirit!

"The word unites you with me and takes you to the spiritual stage of immortality. This alone is therefore genuine nectar and true elixir. This alone transports you to the very core of my life and being. This alone takes you to the innermost recesses of truth and reality. This alone gives you eternal bliss and beatitude.

"The word is real nectar; real wine, but you cannot get its effects by talking or reading or singing. It cannot be described. It is only tasted.

"The mystics are contented only with the real jewel. Religion holds tenaciously to outward ceremonies.

"You can never have true nectar unless you get it from one who possesses it himself. Only the mystics possess this wine of God.

"Only they can give it to others.

"Although the word is within you, the key is with the mystics, the Vairagi adepts.

"Instead of getting the true wine from within, man tries to find it outside in ritual and ceremonies, lakes and rivers, oceans, mountains, birds, insects, trees, stones, moon, stars and all other places.

"Man is ignorant in the darkness. He seeks the nectar at the wrong place. It is within you and if you go to a perfect mystic he will teach you where to find this wine of God, which is within your own temple of being.

"What is truth?

118

"What is absolute truth?

"Absolute truth is that nectar, that wine of God, that divine melody, the name, the word, Bani, music of the spheres, the Qualima, Nad, or whatever word you desire to call it.

"It alone is truth. It cannot die or vanish and lives forever, for all ages and times. It is indestructible and everlasting. It is the truth which was, is and shall be!

"I have finished!"

CHAPTER 9

Saviors in Limbo

It was strange to think that after all this wandering across the planes of God into the regions of the highest realm, that I had not found myself at all.

What got me into this region was a lack of attachment. I had an awful desire for God at one time, then gave it up and in doing so, according to what Rebazar Tarzs said, was able to get into the pure heavens of God.

Briefly, I wish to say that desires start attachment. Afterwhile desire fades and only attachment is left. But sooner or later one will give up attachment and this brings them to the original desire again.

This is the way one reaches God.

Once you form a desire to reach God you start an attachment. When you start the attachment for Him there is no way of getting away from Him. Jesus said, "Once you have put your hands to the plowshare never look back!"

Lot's wife did this and was turned into a pillar of salt. It meant that she was so paralyzed with fear that she was made solid with her emotions.

We all, now and then, become paralyzed with fear for we do not anticipate where God is leading us; and whether we are on the right path, and if this is really God; do we have the right teacher, and hundreds of similar questions of this nature.

All of these doubts plague the seekers.

The best way to tell you how to give up attachment is to become indifferent -- a very fine point of indifference. It is not really an attitude of indifference in the way we think in the Occidental world, but with that poise of mind that you see, understand and know, and cannot be bothered with, is what has taken place.

When I became aware of the environment again Rebazar Tarzs and I were sitting on the side of a rocky trail near an escarpment, stretching across the horizon as far as the eye could see. It was a black frozen wilderness in the midst of a vast desert.

The walls rose black and forlorn into the sky, and over it came a hot wind blowing a strange humming sound, that Sound which belonged to the higher worlds -- the sound of Bani. The Voice of God.

Time passed and then out of the desert came a tiny figure riding a camel. It grew and grew until it became a man in a dark, flopping robe and black, broad brimmed hat. He was an incredibly strong-looking man, big and virile with the strength of God showing in his limbs, body and face. His mouth was a line without lips, his eyes deep crevices, in the bottom of which was the faint gleam of humor. His hands were granite, but strong, beautiful hands.

He halted the camel. The tinkling bells of its harness stopped as he slid off and bowed.

"You are welcome to this land, friends," said a deep resonant sound that hummed out of him. "I, Shamus-i-Tabriz, greet you!"

This was the great Shamus-i-Tabriz, teacher of the mystic poet Jalalu'd din Rumi, of Persia, one of the milestones in the mystical history of all mankind. He lived on earth during the thirteenth century and knew all things, all that one should know about God. Now he was here on some mystic plane in the cosmic universe of God.

"We have been to the Sugmad," said Rebazar Tarzs.

"He has become the Anami?" Shamus questioned looking at me. "Then he should know all things, but I see by the light around him there are many things yet that he needs to know before being accepted into the ancient order of the Bourchakoun!"

"He will know," replied Rebazar Tarzs.

"There are times for all things, says the Christian Bible," Shamus remarked seating himself. "No man, nor Soul ever reaches the fulfillment of the quest for God. One goes on and on and on throughout all eternity, deeper into perfection and deeper into God. You understood this when I was your master," he said to Rebazar Tarzs who nodded. "You will never find God by searching for Him. He is here and now within you! So never search. Just realize this!"

For a moment the strange eyes closed. Then they opened again, fixed upon me. "I am very old," he said, "older than time, wiser than Souls. Here in this world between heaven and the dual worlds, I have spent my time helping those Souls who are lost; who have not the courage to make their way into the true region of Muqam-I-Hag.

"Do you hear it?"

I sat motionless listening to the wind. "Yes, I hear the sound of the winds!"

"There is no wind, young one. That is Akash-Bani, the Voice of God! Some call it Kalami-l-Lahi, a Moslem word for the sound current.

"Time is nothing here. The stillness here is the faint murmuring of that voice which is now occurring within Soul. All men can hear it if they stop and listen. Only some more clearly than others.

"But when most men stop to listen, they hear only

123

the growling of an overstuffed stomach, the pounding of a heart quickened by the pretty shape of a woman; the rattle of wine in their entrails, or the roar of blood in their brains.

"Ah, all men are fools in their earthly form if they have not heard the Bani roaring through their hearts.

"What is sex?

"Only a form of lower communication between man and woman! Man says things with his sexual behavior patterns, to himself, to his parents, to his society, such as 'Look here, I am a normal Soul,' or many trivial things that without thinking they are invariably saying 'Look here I am God, but I don't dare say so!'

"Man uses sex as a weapon in many roles on earth. It has been used to seal political empires and business together. It is always used to attain prestige or status in society. It is, in a few persons, merely a means of getting a family. It is used to express contempt and to express tenderness and love.

"It is used to protest or punish. Man may tell his mate that he loves her, but by his sexual behavior shows that he does not.

"Man uses it as a form of feeling to express to himself that he is a member of the human race.

"Many men live a useful life with it or without it. It is, in a way, a normal function of God's gift to man, and the best of it is that which is integrated into a man's overall life, without undue dependence on it in any way of living out the earthly life.

"It is the highest aspect of sex that it should be an aspect of pleasure and not for anything else. Only one out of every million, of men, will put it in this category.

"Man feels the need for synthesis, the need to avoid the intellectual and emotional conflicts which has puzzled the Occidentals during the last two centuries on earth. The apparent conflicts between matter and spirit, between science and mysticism.

"The Occidental scientist thought he had solved the problem when he had either denied the existence of spirit and of psychic phenomena, or admitted two entirely separate universes, one of which would be unknown, out of reach during his lifetime and would remain the preservation of dogmatic religion.

"Man is at least searching for the synthesis, for the integration of various unrelated or conflicting portions of human knowledge, that led to God knowledge, instead of denying the reality of what does not fit into his personal conception of the Cosmic.

"In a sense, Christianity has failed mankind but it is now beginning to see light and the true teachings are gradually making headway in the west. Man hardly knew anything about Eckankar, the secret science of Soul Travel, or about Bani, until the Eshwar-Khanewale adepts started making their presence felt in the world of man.

"Faith in the dogma has been the motto of the Christian churches. Faith in the Word of God has been the teachings of the adepts.

"The science of Eckankar is, the Spiritual Travelers, Bani, which is the music of God, and Jivan Mukti, the spiritual freedom here and now. Perfect liberation during this lifetime.

"These six words sum up the complete teachings of the travelers. They are the three blazing truths, combined to put together the greatest system of truth ever revealed to the consciousness of man. They are like the three mighty peaks of Sahasra-dal-Kanwal in Tirkuti, (the astral world) which are grouped together to form one gigantic mountain of light.

"These are the essence of the path of the spiritual travelers and stand out in blazing light to the very entrance in the start of the royal highway leading upward into Anami Lok.

"The sequence of these three truths of God are

fixed by law. It is not chance that they come in the order as they are, but must never be tampered with nor modified. The traveler comes first, for he is the Guru, or teacher, second, Bani or Word, and third is Jivan Mukti.

"Salvation is sought by all men. But the salvation which I speak of is different in letter and law than that which is known to the mind of man. The salvation of the traveler is liberation from the Wheel of the Eighty-Four, from all ills of the mortal life, and the ability to come and go among the worlds of the Cosmic order as desired.

"This is spiritual freedom!

"The blind faith of religions is never good for man. The Christian councils, as well as the Moslems, Buddhists, and other religions, crushed the gnostic believers in reincarnation and advocates of esoteric knowledge in the fifth to the eighth world century and blind faith in their leaders became the supreme argument of religions in their respective worlds. Slowly and gradually the energies of all religions have been diverted toward the physical world and the same rational and experimental approach built up by the physical science which has helped build spiritual knowledge among the mystics of the East.

"A basic difference exists between the two knowledges, a difference which must be taken into account when trying to apply scientific methods to spiritual techniques. Knowledge of the Sugmad, God, has but one aim, the opportunity to help Soul discover the Ultimate Reality, the Word of God, or Truth.

"Man is free to choose whatever method he wishes in order to achieve this aim, whether it be purely a spiritual method of a righteous and selfless life, or the way of the spiritual travelers who will give you the shortest way into the Supreme Ocean of Love and Mercy.

"The way is a long one unless the seekers will by accident, or by the pull of Soul's desire, bring himself into the presence of the living teacher. If he chooses other methods to seek this approach into the heavenly kingdom of love and mercy then he will spin on the wheel of transmigration through eternity until one day he will meet with a spiritual traveler.

"The work that he has done to gain liberation is not entirely lost for it helps to bring him closer to the traveler. Every perfection of himself brings one nearer to the divine sonship, as does the making of honey by the flower bud draw the bee eventually to it.

"Without the help of the traveler no man can ever gain permanent relief from the wheel of birth and death. Their eternal motion must go on until their good karma earn them the right to meet the traveler.

"Why?

"Because the three links in the golden chain of spiritual freedom must be observed. You cannot get the sound current without the traveler, and neither can you get spiritual liberation without the Word. So you must first meet with the teacher.

"He will help you to connect up with the divine Voice of God. None have ever been refused. This is because all who come to the travelers are ready or they would never have been placed in the path of these great adepts.

"You must first find a real Satguru, or spiritual traveler, an agent of God who can tune you in with the Word, the sound current, and merge yourself into it. It takes one onward and upward into the heights of spiritual freedom. When you have passed the frontiers of the cosmic worlds into the real ocean of love and mercy you have perfect freedom, and can come and go as desired across those borders from the lowest world to the highest.

"This is spiritual freedom!

"The traveler makes certain that the chela is ready and can be entrusted with the knowledge that he will gain by his travels into the higher worlds. This is necessary because of the great powers acquired by the chela.

"This connection between knowledge and moral standards is the distinctive feature of all science and esoteric teachings, a secret technique which is handed down from one high teacher to another, as in the secret order of the adepts spoken about earlier. It comes down by word of mouth or written in such symbolic terms as to be incomprehensible to the reader who is not able to grasp the meaning.

"Would anyone believe that Whitman's Leaves of Grass is a scripture? Of course not. But man is the worm that crawls on its belly until the Bani in him is aroused, then he becomes the soaring eagle.

"And would anyone believe that my writings are a scripture? Of course not. But man is the serpent that seeks to feed upon insects until at last the Bani is aroused in him; then he becomes the beautiful nightingale.

"Two principles in the occidental world of matter now constitute the complete knowledge of the physical science of men. They are the Quantum Theory, dealing with the constitution of matter and energy and the Einstein Theory of Relativity which covers modern conception of time, space and the universe. Indeed a very limited knowledge.

"Man is now learning that he has reached definite limits, barriers beyond which he cannot proceed in the physical. It is slowly dawning upon him that beyond are the great psychical worlds in which his scientific laws and methods are worthless.

"Matter is nothing more than condensed energy. It is made up of electrical waves proceeding out of the

128

heart of God and these waves are the light and energy which is Bani, the Word of God; for all things are made of the Word!

"All then is in error!

"Man knows nothing!

"The gods know nothing.

"Then who knows anything? The travelers know. God gives the knowledge to His supreme sons who come into the lower worlds to impart to those who seek for it.

"After they have given all, they come to this plane to dwell, for like man there is nothing for them to do elsewhere, nor anyone with whom to further discuss the Word of God, and no place for them to go. Hence, you might say that this is the place where the 'Saviors are in Limbo!'

"If you would look about they are found: St. John of the Cross, Buddha, St. Paul, Hafiz, Rumi, Rama, Vishnu and hundreds of others. Many that you never heard of, and none upon the earth have even had ideas that such Souls existed at anytime. Remember the great Mexican God Quetzacoatl? He is here. That is one example — there are many others here.

"For what reason are they congregated here? This is home to them. They live here over behind that great escarpment; the home of the spiritual travelers. They make the laws of the universal worlds and they see that all things are kept in order for God.

"They don't live like man does on earth. Maybe someday Rebazar Tarzs will take you to this mysterious city, but not this time.

"Man has free right to choose his own actions, but he must balance these actions with equal and opposite reactions until he learns that God's one law must be obeyed. This God holds inviolable.

"The whole purpose of life is to learn how to manifest God in Truth and the Law. The lesson is hard but man himself makes it hard by his ignorance of the law. As man gradually knows his purpose in life and the law by knowing God in himself, his life becomes more and more beautiful; and man gains more power in his manifestation of power.

"The power of man lies in giving. He must learn to give as nature (or God) gives. Each half of a cycle of the wave from Bani eternally gives to the other half for re-giving. God forever unfolds into many for the purpose of refolding into the one. Each thing must manifest this universal law of God.

"So man must know the principle of God; giving between each interchanging opposite half of each cycle for the purpose of repeating its giving. This is the law of the audible life stream, the sound current, the Bani, or the Word of God, and everything, every being must manifest this law.

"The outstanding characteristic of the waves in the sound current is that they are forever interchanging; the going out and the returning. This division of light (really the sound) into a seeming two is manifested in the universal body of God by electric waves of two opposing lights springing up from the still sea of God's Word, just as waves of water spring from the calm ocean.

"The troughs become crests and crests become troughs. So long as quality of interchanges continue rhythmically, waves repeat their interchanges. When the sloping sand at the beach prevents this equality of rhythmic balanced interchange, the waves accumulate unbalance until they crash on the shore.

"The same happens in the inner worlds so that the unbalanced waves of the sound will crash upon the atmosphere of a cosmic region, place or world.

"The pulse beat of God, the swinging pendulum, the inbreathing and the outbreathing of living things, all exemplify God's one law of rhythmical balanced inter-

130

change based upon the sound current. Any deviation from that law in the heart beat of a man, or a world, physical or cosmic, will endanger the continuance of that thing, but where there is a rhythmic balanced interchange between the two compression and expansion opposites, man's life, the life of a universe continues to function at its maximum.

"Despite this, man's disobedience to the law cannot affect the balance of man in his whole journey for every unbalanced action of his must eventually be balanced. All the storms of the world cannot effect the balance of the earth, for the balance in the universe cannot be upset. The earth continues in its fixed, balanced orbit with so much precision that its position can be determined at any time to the split second.

"You understand now?

"Man is on his way to his cosmic goal of oneness with the great God of all things, and he can in no way deviate from that fixed orbit which will eventually take him to his destination of glory in the higher heavens.

"The empty space of the cosmic worlds welded onto empty time characterizes the spiritual kingdom — worlds which cannot be defined and studied scientifically from the viewpoint of man, for he has not developed, intuitively, a world which is not billions of light years away but around you constantly; worlds in which the only reality are waves of sound current. You can then conceive that on the edge of this spiritual world, the crystallization of thought-consciousness had produced the physical universe in a small portion of which man spends his short earthly life.

"Now it is easier to understand the basic difference between the introverted mystic viewpoint who can see the entire physical-spiritual continuum, the real universe from the inside, and the scientist who calculates it from the exterior side. Only the spiritual traveler who has reached the highest degree of spiritual insight, who has been able to still His mechanical brain and develop his super intuition, can see that the universe is the non-dimensional continuum which the physical scientists are slowly discovering and in which the only reality is the action of the sound-current and spirit.

"Since the spirit is the sole reality, the study of it must become essential.

"Even though man knows so little from where to start it seems that we go back to where we started in the beginning. This is the search for the teacher or the traveler.

"In doing so just where does man go in order to find the teacher?

"This is very simple!

"Go inside yourself!

"Not strange at all, for even in your own particular case did not Rebazar Tarzs appear to you many times before you met him in the physical flesh?

"The traveler knows who must come to him, and begins to prepare that Soul to meet with him. This great Soul, who is carrying you through this experience was seven years with his master, myself, before he saw me in flesh. I spent years with my master in the same experience and Rumi knew me before we met.

"This is true of all those who seek God.

"There are three things of supreme importance to anyone who is desirous of the path to God. They are: the spiritual traveler, or teacher, the meeting with the teacher in the other worlds, also in the flesh, and the sound current.

"He must first meet with the spiritual traveler, but when he comes to him, then the neophyte must attend Satsang. This means that he must converse with the traveler, or Guru, listen to His discourses, and get filled with instruction. He may not ever attend

132

any public meetings like church, and group gatherings, but the point is that he must see enough of the Guru to become well informed as to the great truths of the Path.

"This prepares the seeker for entering the path. After this he is ready for the vital contact with the life stream, or Word of God.

"By doing this the seeker eventually becomes self-sufficient unto himself and the teacher sends him out into the world to do for himself, perhaps to teach others and be of his own world. Yet the teacher will never leave the seeker. He will be with him, in the Atma Sarup, at all times, as in the past, during the lifetime of the seeker, and helps him during all difficulties and trials and troubles.

"And in the final stage gives the seeker the true spiritual freedom!

"Do you understand?"

134

CHAPTER 10

Fierce Children of Light

itting there in the light I could not think anymore. Nothing seemed right. According to the
standards of the planet earth and mankind
everything was wrong.

In this state I was wondering if anyone knew
anything; did Bacon, Shopenhauer, Tulsi Das, Omar
Khayyám, Sri Aurobindo, Gandhi, Burke, Newton,
Shaw, Kabir, Mohammed, Swinburne, Swedenborg,
Fox, St. James, Capenter, Augustine or any of the
great thinkers? I am not sure that they did.

I thought about all the thousands of books which I
had read on all subjects of philosophy, religion and
metaphysics in practically every library in the world,
and my talks with the spiritual greats in both flesh
and spirit. Yet they all came up with something that
was puzzling.

That was the entities which surround and bother
man so much, and for what reason.

I mustered sufficient strength to ask: "Oh Sri Tarzs,
what of those little elements that walk through my
sleep? What of those entities that ride the waves of
God through the universe?"

Rebazar Tarzs smiled and looked at me with humor

shining in his great eyes. He listened patiently to my questions.

"I would think that you would be satisfied with the experience of traveling through the eight worlds and seeing God, the ultimate experience of all!" he smiled lightly. "Most Souls who get such trips are happy with what I have done for them!"

I replied, "Shamus was right! No man knows everything!"

He laughed shaking the little world where we were sitting. "Jinns, fairies and demons," he remarked smilingly. "I guess you will be getting around to flying saucers next?"

"Now that you reminded me, yes!"

"Why do you want to be bothered?" he asked seriously. "You don't need flying machines to get to the other planets in the lower universes. You just project yourself there!"

"Really? What about all those flying saucers and the things that everybody keeps talking about?"

"Like what?"

"Messages from space people!"

"Mostly psychic junk, but some of it is true," said Rebazar Tarzs. "Some of the people on other planets need mechanical vehicles to move about the universe. But many of the highly spiritual don't. They project between planets. You will have this information soon enough. However, there are occasions when the astral entities pierce the veil between the worlds and play tricks with people and make them think there are flying saucers and such things around. Some times there are but often there aren't.

"There are authentic cases of flying saucers and space people, but now that it has become a fad among the homo sapiens, some of the astral entities have seized upon it to be a part of their pranks they play on men's mechanical brain. They do this by telling

136

men that they are space people and have a message for whomever will listen.

"If the receiver is at all psychic the entity can put on a real show, assuming the strange garb of some weird exotic costume, appearing before the victim of its prank and jibber a wild message. The entity might also conjur up a space ship and by illusion put the victim inside for a trip, and for a short time that person might walk among the people of another planet and see sights not recorded by the human brain, but it is all illusion created by a powerful entity for a real joke on some poor human.

"This very entity is likely to go back to his old astral haunts, gather up his friends and put on a roaring party in which he describes his adventures with humans. Those with any sort of ability get the same idea and go out to find a human victim on which to play practical jokes.

"Then suddenly many in the human form will be running around with a great deal of clatter about receiving messages from space people. The government tells its people who have been contacted that this is crazy, but those people are sure their government was keeping something from them about space people. A friction develops between the people and their government. Newspaper editorials are written against the government heads and the people grow restless and angry over their supposed suppression of truth. Sooner or later their anger breaks out into a rage against authority in conventional channels and the first thing we know there is a small rebellion going on; maybe not with guns, but milder yet dangerous for the regime in power.

"You can be assured that the entities are laughing hard over the trouble they have started among the humans. It is merely a practical joke to them, and a good one if you stop to think about it."

"Can this sort of thing be stopped?"

"It is constantly being handled. When an entity over-reaches its conduct behavior in the other world it is taken into custody by others in the same manner as a policeman does in the earth world. There are jails in the lower psychic worlds as well as on the physical planes. Your system of law there is taken from the similar system on the astral plane.

"The police in the lower astral worlds have a different way of handling their law breakers than you do. In the first place they do not need a large force to patrol their planes as in the physical world. They have machines made of astral fabrics which record the wave lengths of each world, and each area within the various astral planes.

"When anything goes wrong the astral force can spot it instantly and track down the culprit almost at once.

"There are times when something goes wrong in the astral world, which are so cleverly devised by a gang of psychic criminals, on a large scale upon the population of either the physical or astral world that it gets by the police's detecting machines. But it will never escape the Lord of that Universe who will send out commands to take the psychic thugs into custody. This is done at once!

"Sometimes the Lord of a particular plane on which this happens with catch the misdemeanor at once and take care of it.

"For your information, the Lord of the physical world, meaning rather the first astral plane, who governs the physical world in its hierarchy has many names: Jehovah by the Jews; Ganesh by the Hindus; Malcuth by the Kabbalah; Adonai ha Aretz by the Moslems. But it is the same God ruling the same world under Jot Niranjan. There are six planes, corresponding to the actual spinal centers below the neck and which are psychic worlds, and each have a ruler. These are the psychic worlds, of the chakras which many Hindu teachers base their teachings upon and when opened start problems for the devotees, real psychic problems and strangely cannot be handled by the teacher."

I said, "Now I can see that there is order instead of confusion on the other side of the veil of life. We are not exactly at the mercy of the psychic criminals as we are always led to believe by the spiritualist mediums?"

"That is right," he replied. "Nobody can harm you in any stage of your development or travels unless you let them. Not even the Lords of the cosmic planes could do anything if they desire; which is never likely."

He continued slowly, "Yes, you will know more about this eventually. In fact you should know everything about this particular subject for the simple reason that mystery is a mystery until knowledge enters into your consciousness and then you have understanding. The psychic is not harmful to man, as he is led to believe, but very helpful, yet it is not something that one would consider to be the means to an end. It is just that if we would get too interested here, it would be found that the psychic has all kinds of traps to keep the mind occupied and keeps one from developing.

"This is why you should know about it. To keep you from falling into traps that could spring up along the way to the true kingdom.

"If one has protection of the spiritual travelers then no harm can come to him. That is unless he endeavors to do something by his own efforts and voluntarily against my warning. He could fall into a trap and stay there until the traveler decides to let

139

him out. I might do it immediately and again I might take my time."

He continued. "If you had no training in this particular field it might be that several traps could be laid for you. And before I forget, some time soon you will have to strike out alone in these worlds. It is only natural since you have reached the area of spiritual training which requires no traveler to go along with you.

"Many neophytes are required to go into training in complete darkness to learn what are hallucinations and what are not. During my training I too underwent this kind of test. My Guru locked me in a dark room where I meditated for weeks on the gradual weeding out of unnecessary thoughts to achieve one-pointedness, the perfect concentration of mind on an idea. This was in another life, of course. All conception of day and night, of space and time disappeared. Absolute solitude brought out vividly the lack of self-control. Visions and mental pictures of all kinds constantly floated around the room.

"A long period and tireless effort were needed to dissolve those phantasmagorias and mirages. But gradually, I replaced these visions with a small moving spot which gradually reduced in size to that of a minute point and disintegrated it completely.

"Then I began a number of spiritual exercises which the Guru kept sending me, guiding me by mental telepathic messages until I was on the right path. Through constant meditation I eliminated sleep and became free from the perpetual cycle of effort relaxation to which ordinary men are subjected. I became one continuous effort toward enlightenment.

"The little self faded and in time I acquired what you call super-human powers; one of the first steps toward mastership. Perhaps the easiest achievements

140

are the creation of forms, perhaps you call them ghosts which became reality, that can move, do anything and be at my command. They would last until their psychic energies were dissipated. So you see I could have companionship if necessary. Many of these things I learned, but only as a means to learn God.

"You can do without them if necessary, however, sometime you may have need of them. So I will give you the experience. Gobind Singh, tenth Guru, in the line of successors for Guru Nanak, and St. Theresa, of the Christian religion, are among those who had powers like this. They are among the many who have lived in darkness to find God.

"The saint Shiv Dayal Singh ji, spent seventeen years in meditation in a dark room before he gave out his first public lecture.

"Now let me get back to the original subject."

He continued, "One of the things which I developed after becoming a teacher was the art of invisibility at will. I learned how to move among humans without arousing the slightest suspicion or sensations among them. No perception took place and not even the subconscious of the spectators could register my presence around them. I became proficient at this science of transferring one's consciousness from one mind to another, from one body to another.

"The deep purpose of my efforts were never overlooked. These psychic achievements were nothing but stepping stones toward God, nothing but illusions of the sangsaric world. I made greater effort toward Godhood. Having greater compassion for all those who lived and suffered.

"Gradually, I left behind the world of phenomenon, not only to the world of the earth, but the psychic and superhuman powers and began, under my master's tutorage, the study of the Void, in the plane of Daswan

141

Dwar, climbing the endless spiraling path which leads beyond the mystic visions and transcends objects of joy or suffering, finite or infinite, time or eternity, existence, or non-existence, to the Void where those terms are meaningless, toward the Ultimate Reality. Words, as you well realize by now, are useless; they cannot express the inexpressable.

"Of course such transcendental illumination cannot and never will be communicated; it can only be experienced.

"A true master of the spiritual worlds will never allow himself to make a public exhibition of his powers. Never expect me to act like the many fakirs of India and the pseudo-magicians you find in Tibet."

He paused and after while said again, "It is against the law of God to do so!"

I stared at Rebazar Tarzs, neither moving nor speaking. His head nodded gently, the great black eyes closed a moment then snapped open again.

"Now has come the time to show you," he said. "In this world where the life of the psyche flows freely. Here you can see the fierce children of light and their creator — the terrible things they do to one another. In time you will find these children are of our own making."

Once more the lids closed over his beautiful eyes. He sat unmoved, his head upward in the light. His face was utterly inhuman. It was old, yet it was not old; it was old like a tree, a rock, the waters of the sea, the sands of the desert, with a terrible ageless majesty and calmness. The moments passed and I sat watching him, and I watched as the rush of the wind passing through the boughs of the trees overhead, broke the silence. It was really not the wind but the sound current.

That was all there was in this world, the wind and

the sound. All there was inside myself was the thundering and revolving.

And before me was the ancient mark of the Holy Lama.

I heard myself saying, "Is it necessary?"

His lids opened again. "Yes, it is necessary," said his voice.

It seemed that I ceased to breathe and that my heart was no longer there; all that was left was a dim consciousness, transfixed and imprisoned. I struggled to break away from this prison.

"I am ready," I said.

"Of course," he replied in words that tore at my spiritual flesh, and hung in the air. A sound rose and closed in around us howling wildly. It was no longer a thing outside me, but within, a part of me, inside like a beating tom-tom. I said quickly. "Are you with me, Sire?"

Only a stillness. Then blackness.

I became conscious of a growing light. Suddenly it was discovered that the light was with me growing ever greater, and greater, until it was a mighty arc-lamp, spreading out into the universe. I saw that light was my body, and that all light was my body, and that all was within that world, people, growing things and minerals and that all life in my world was made from the fabric of my body.

My consciousness was in the center of this light and yet it was in the things that dwelled therein.

I thought, and that thought became a reality, a thing in my world, and then it grew legs, arms, head and body and came forth into life!

The power of Agam Lok!

Behold I was the Lord of a world. Just where this universe was I did not know but I was the ruler and absolute creator of everything that took place in it.

There were angels, minor deities, and creatures of the lower orders, the four elemental entities, Gnomes of the earth; the Undines of the sea; the Sylphs of the air, and the Salamanders of the fire.

I always thought of them as happy creatures but they were at one another fighting. Hatred dominated them. Fierce battles raged through the spiritual ethers of my universal body. The creatures were at war, killing, looting and raping.

There was no peace in this world of mine. I knew the reason, for as Lord of this world there was a power coming out of the world above which was a stronger negative nature than of a positive. I had to overcome this in some manner or other — but then it was realized that this was the lower negative pole and I had to receive this power in this manner.

I, God, the creator was the power. There was no power other than mine in this world, and all the energy which my creatures floated upon came out of my consciousness, the center of the majestic light, the true light of Soul.

When one of the creatures thought, then he had all the power that I, the father-mother, thinker of the creation in this world, had. In this world of my mind was the desire to give creative expression to that one single ideal by thinking it into parts. Desire, as I saw it now, was Soul of the mind and the will of mind. Desire in the light of my mind was the power quality of mind.

The expression of power to create ideas as products now lay in the electric action of thinking ideas at rest in the light of the mind, in two lights of motion which simulated the idea.

All expression of energy sprung from the ocean of stillness and calm within my heart. It sought a point of rest and return to the condition of resting in the ocean again.

144

As God I was the fulcrum of my creatures and of the universe in the body. Neither the creatures nor any moving thing in my universe had power within itself to do anything except through me. All power expressed by man was channeled directly from the Father within me to the father-mother light of the earth and heavens which originally manifested him.

The mechanical principle, by means of which power is expressed by myself as Creator, was in the light of a two-way motion which recorded two-way cycles which were divided equally to express the two desires of the power to create form images out of the mind power and to destroy those forms sequentially for reforming.

Waves of motion sprang up from the stillness of the universal ocean. They were the universal heartbeat which manifested eternal life and power in my stillness by eternal repetitions of simulated life and power as expressed in waves of motion.

There was no place in my world where there was not life. The whole body was made up of cells of light and this light was the atoms of the universal Soul. They were alive, filled with intelligence, power and love.

Below was the hierarchy of my kingdom. I had three sons who were known as Brahma, Vishnu and Shiva, the three giant streams of subordinate powers. They sprang from the union of myself with the mother power and had charge of the lower kingdom. Below them was the king of the lower world Ganesh who ruled over the devas, devtas, bhuts, prets, generally called angels and the four elementals as previously named.

These existed in the kingdom of my universal body!

But there were other creatures, ugly, malignant, terrible creatures that floated out of the mind stream of the brain into this world. Invisible creatures

145

to man, that attacked and drove him into insanity, into poverty, into hideous crimes and negative things which he would never have done under normal conditions.

This was of my doing, of my own nature. The attack upon my own beautiful creatures — warring against my own children. My children? Yes, these terrible creatures were my own children, too.

They were of my own creation. Yes, this was true. I was creating them through the negative stream, through hated and mechanical habits of the negative nature. It was a stupefying thought but true. A thought that almost staggered the imagination yet it was actual truth and there was no denying it. As God I attacked my own with my own. But why?

The answer was very simple!

As God of my universe, as creator of my own world, I was not free. I created because it was compulsive and mechanical, a part of my nature, and not understanding the true aspect of imagination it had gone on for years without any control over it. I had created these thought creatures of hideous nature through hatred, jealousy and ill will. They at the time had gained control of the emotional nature.

All of which now became very plain.

Before anyone can reach God, or find the Ultimate Reality, he must learn the art of mind control. Too many think of this in the terms of putting a clamp on their thoughts. It would drive one crazy to do this sort of control. But to gain complete control of the mind, there must be a much simpler way. If you have a series of words representing the sounds of the various planes it is simpler to turn the mind to these words whenever needed to control the thoughts. Secondly, if you have been tuned-in by a spiritual traveler like Rebazar Tarzs, to the sound current, then you just turn the attention to it which is always flowing through you and listen.

These will clean out those malignant children of light, those fierce entities which destroy mankind in a devilish work which is a part of man's own karma to have created them.

However, if one doesn't have a spiritual traveler in his life there is another way, and that is by picture control of thoughts; by thinking in pictures instead of words we can get a better control of the thoughts. By shifting of the pictures in the mind to something more pleasant, then that which is of a negative nature will disappear.

Getting rid of the thought children is easier this way than any other method except to raise one's self from the lower consciousness. These small entities are the things which have bothered man throughout his earthly life, and are able to create all kinds of obstacles. Yet they are of man's own making, as was shown to me during this part of my journey through the cosmic worlds.

Shortly I came back to consciousness again and found Rebazar Tarzs, laughing silently. He knew what I had experienced for He had been with me all the time witnessing what had taken place and the experiences that were mine — uniquely mine.

"Now you know," he said.

I nodded slowly, "Yes, I know."

He laughed again quietly, silently. Afterwhile he stopped laughing and grew silent.

CHAPTER 11

The Worship of Moloch

here is a verse in the book of the Shariyat Ki Sugmad, the Way of The Eternal, which is the ancient scripture of the Eckankar, that goes like this, "Death pursues life. Is there anything without its opposite? Or any cause without its consequence? Or any light that casts no shadow?

"So it's known that your very innermost thoughts awaken hosts that had slept, as sound awakens echoes. Therefore it is neither miracle nor mystery that there is no escape from the spires nor safety other than as upright zeal, leaving these hosts forever behind.

"This is the so-called mystery of leadership!"

This explains how one gets into the kingdom of God. Arouse the curiosity for God and one will always have to be out in front of the crowd, seeking God first, and knowing that every living thing in the universe is watching. Not even your innermost secrets are hidden from anything or anybody.

However, there is a warning to all who are ignorant of this fact. Do not under any circumstances ever become angry with anyone who is high on the spiritual survival scale, or with the Spiritual Travelers, criticize them for any fault, or be against them, deride them in anyway, or belittle them. If you do you are in trouble.

The true spiritual traveler is not a man. He is the agent of God, the representative of the spiritual light, the cosmic light, of itself. This is truth within itself.

If you should ever ask the spiritual traveler for help you would likely get silence. If he should agree to help, you might then say afterwards that he did not help you...because you know nothing of the methods he used.

The surgeon's knife helps but the patient protests bitterly against the pain. So if the spiritual traveler, or the teacher promises to help, take advantage of his promise. This is human nature but in the end you would be relying on him instead of using your own ability. Whereas it is only when you have put forth absolutely all of your own ability that he can help you.

Do not be surprised if the teacher would open the door for you through which you would step and then close the same door behind you, in the face of your best friends and nearest relatives. Yet there would be nothing, no word, not even a gesture on your part, not so much as a hint in the change in relationship. The only way others might find out would be a feeling experienced in the same manner as a wife who sees a pretty girl approach her husband in a confidential manner and realize the feeling that went between them.

You can never expect anything from the teacher except benevolence.

"Moloch," said Rebazar Tarzs, "Do you know what the worship of Moloch is?"

I shook my head.

"Moloch was a pagan God for one of the ancient races in the Middle East, long before Christ. It was represented by a gigantic metal monster that took in through its maws money, gems, wealth of all kinds and even pretty virgins, during a ritual. It was a dishonest practice of religion with the people — done by the priestcraft."

We were walking through a forest and stopped by a blue, bubbling spring to drink of its cold waters.

When I got up from my knees from drinking the water, there standing beside me was a wonderful looking man with a long, gray beard, a fez and deep brown eyes. He must have been in his late sixties, square built, about five feet nine inches tall, and had a square face.

"This is My Lord, Fubbi Quantz," said Rebazar Tarzs. "He is one of the great travelers from the city of Agam Des, the greatest of spiritual cities on the Earth planet."

The magnificent being smiled sweetly. "You were speaking of Moloch, Tibetan? Is it not true that man is still inflicted with the same terrible disease? The worship of personality? Of the personality cults?"

"This is true, My Lord," replied Rebazar Tarzs.

"The true teachings never emphasize the form, but the formless. Neither does the true teachings ever interfer with the individual freedom, any more than God interfers with man's free will. The greatest good for all prevails always. The secret of God has always been a secret until discovered by the individual. He is just as secret to man today as electricity was to Thales, Gilbert, Faraday and all others following them, who individually discovered just a little about electricity. It has always been there but Edison had to find it, and having found it workable, gave it to the world, to use or misuse. Yet electricity was not confined to the world. Neither is God confined to one world.

"What has this got to do with the worship of Moloch?" I asked.

The reverend master explained. "If you worshipped

man, then you are worshipping Moloch. If you worship the personality you are worshipping Moloch. Compare this with what I am telling you.

"If you would look beneath all things, God is to be found. Worship God in the many!"

"Why has God been kept a secret?" I asked.

"Who has kept the secret of God?" he replied. "The priestcraft, of course. But was there any need for man to keep it from himself? He could have investigated and found one of us, the spriritual travelers. No, he was too busy, engaged in murdering his neighbors, ever to look for God. He was too superstitious to dare make any attempt, afraid of being mocked or burnt for heresy. Even today nine-tenths of men will mock you if you speak of the existence of God, and the remainder will try to put you in a mental asylum. Some will curse you in the name of their religions, and some will believe you for selfish reasons. Selfishness prevents discovery of anything worth while. Look at inventions. No worthwhile discovery has been made by those working solely for profit. Those who have brought forth something for their fellowman have found that the greatness of the discovery has paralleled the degree of unselfishness of the discoverer.

"Selfishness makes people mentally blind. That is a scientific fact. Look at this!"

The forest around us suddenly changed into a cinerama of pictures, of a great scene where stood a monstrous, hideous brass head, on a platform higher than treetops, and surrounded by a flaming inferno. And around the brass head were dancing women, completely nude, except for oriental headdresses. Guarding them were white robed priests with headbands that had a serpent's head reared up in front.

Millions of frenzied screaming people surrounded the altar shouting for their great God Moloch to help them. Occasionally a nude dancer would leap into the

152

open maws of the brass creature screaming, to disappear into a flame of fire.

"Moloch!" said Fubbi Quantz, "was a worthless worship. Completely black magic at its worse. A set of spiritual criminals making use of the Kal power in its crudest way. That is what you call Satan, the devil, Lucifer, Mammon, Baal, demonism, black mass, witchcraft, or anything you like to call it. Until man became aware that God was within himself such practices continued, in every land in every universe!"

Fascinated I watched the scene while he talked, "I warn you that you must always go forward. You cannot turn back now, no more than Galileo could, once he made his discovery. I speak of the physical impossibility — as for instance putting a chick back into its egg. I will try to explain for the crossing of the Himalayas would be much easier than the task any seeker undertakes once he sets out to discover God. It is physical — absolutely physical, but not as you understand physics.

"If you fully exhaust yourself in one field of endeavor and resign, ready to give up, one day you will awaken to find yourself interested, refreshed and ready to take on another duty. Like retiring from your business worn out and unable to work any longer, then suddenly take up another work, your health gets better and you have new interests in life.

"It only proves that you have exhausted your energies in something that had no further possibilities for your abilities and you could not return to it and live.

"The same holds true when you start seeking God. You can never return to your old world and live there happily. Perhaps you could have lived out your life there to its fullest conclusion, but not likely. When you decided to go forward, you have first to prove that you are fitted to discover what you seek; and there is no way to prove that except by doing it. Like men engaged in an experiment with unknown forces, you will be in constant danger, maybe to your life, and to your earning ability and to your moral reputation.

"In spite of all danger, you make your greatest discovery of the secret of God, and then evolve into a higher spiritual stature. But can you think of any man who ever discovered anything worth while who has not had to cope with mysterious obstructions placed in his path?

"It is like going uphill. There is a law of gravity against us. The desire to go uphill to discover God, that is the impulse of life, and there are those who constantly study the laws which govern it. Those are the ones whom you must learn of, although we never become friends in the social sense of man.

"The downhill pull, the activity of ignorance, prejudice, passion, superstition is the law of death, and there are those who study that, revel in it and identify themselves with it. They are the enemy and are deadly dangerous.

"All men who have made a great discovery have done so in hope of benefiting all humanity. Perhaps the chemist who found poison gas intended it for beneficial use. It is the misuse of the force that makes it evil, and it is possible to misuse any force of God -- forces of electricity, chemistry, religion and thought power.

"Therefore those who study life and who have made discoveries of the many secrets of life, of the universes, of God, are obliged of themselves to guard those secrets because there are others who would use them for evil purposes.

"There are those who study death who are in no less communion with the spiritual forces than those who study life, and are equally wholehearted in their persistence as you can readily understand if you remember how gravity opposes every effort to rise upward. Check the analogy and recall how great teachers have been attacked, vilified and very often murdered.

"If a man makes a great medical discovery the charlatans pounce on him and use it for their own enrichment. Do you now see why they who know God and His secrets are obliged to live in secret and hide their knowledge from the world? They could not dare release their knowledge except to individuals whom they know and trust.

"Morals depend on character, but character never depends on morals. A man's religion never makes any difference. You see this constantly happening in the earth world.

"To pursue evil, man must have evil tendencies which will increase through cultivation as he becomes more responsive to impulses that govern evil.

"Only those who have good character pertaining to the path they choose can succeed in the end; and though a weaver like Kabir can become a poet, that was because he had the poet's nature. In the same way only those who have the necessary character can find God, or be received into the planes of the other worlds.

"Wisdom can neither be bought nor sold, being like a virtue, which, if man or woman should sell it, it could never have been virtue."

"Who are the saints?" I asked curiously.

"Great souls," he said. "Wisdom avoids vanity. Was Lao-Tse vain? Or Bacon? Or Mozart?"

"The saints to themselves, are ordinary men, too fallible, beset by their own perplexities. Our problems are simple to the saints, because they mastered such elementary conditions as ours in former lives; which is why they are called saints. They have advanced to the greater problems.

"Is any contour of a new world quite the same to you, or are the old associations as important? Values have altered as you rise on the spiritual path.

"It is the same with all life, everything is evolving into something else. Would you like to live in the same niche as ten years ago? The difference in that is that you are greater now in your values than of ten years before, in all departments of your life.

"The proof of a man's authority is in its consequence. There is no authority from without. All comes from within. But they are rare who recognize authority, and they are still more rare who have the courage to obey the call from God.

"Truth once released can never be suppressed; although it can be limited and misused. In this case look at Galileo who had only the inner authority for his discovery of the earth movement, and the dishonest officials forbid this. They forced him to recant which he did for he was too sensible to become a martyr and flatter his ego. But his truth had already been released and could never be withdrawn."

I asked, "What happens if a man should see God and fail in his duty?"

"He would never completely see God. He might get very high on the ladder of spiritual success and fail. This is the source for the legend of the fallen angels. It is the same thing as the man who fails as a surgeon, a philosopher, a scientist. Is he not worse than the ignorant if he has envy, hatred and malice in his heart? He becomes dangerous and although the spiritual hierarchy might exclude him, God is always willing to help him return to the path again.

"He might become the leader of the enemies of light, and his lack of integrity excludes him from the society of Saints. It is really only his weight of guilt that holds him off.

"He can call upon the Kal power to seek to justify

himself by deeds. He can use his intelligence to smother light, if that is ever possible, identify himself with all negation and attract to himself all those too unwilling to resist or too stupid to prevent him. See the picture of Moloch there?

"That is the example of what I am speaking of. They will spend age upon age trying to smother truth but failing each time. Rasputin also is an example of this. The western mind of the earth planet being the open mind is subjected to the tragic error of trusting the oriental leaders who seek power behind a mask of peace!

"How can you tell when the Kal power is greater in one man than another? You may say to him 'Bless you' and he will try to use the blessing for a stick with which to beat you. If you say to him, 'This is truth,' he will start working his mind at once to prove it isn't so. If you say 'Love your enemies,' he will go to work to make some enemies, including you first, in order to have someone to love. Show him money and he begins to think how to get that money from you. Make peace in your household, and he will proceed to try to break it up. He thinks vice is a virtue and virtue is a vice.

"Teach man the laws and forces of the universe, and he can turn them against his teacher. Teach me spiritual knowledge and for every one desire to use it rightly, I shall have a thousand impulses to do the wrong thing. Persistence in thinking the right way about God will halt all such impulses.

"At each step of the ladder upward man takes, he must choose all over again on which side of the ladder he will climb. Will he take the virtuous side or the non-virtuous side? For every beam of light there are at once a million shadows and nobody has to tell the shadows where to find the light for they are created by the light, and by the very virtue of the light procreates non-virtue. Moreover the shadow would smother virtue if it could.

"The true spiritual traveler is He who knows that nothing can be taught, although the leader easily can be assisted to discover what is in himself. Other than this there is no knowledge of importance, except that which is in himself is everywhere.

"When the saint meets with the true chela they know one another. How do they know? Tell me how does the horseman know a good horse, or the hunting dog know the huntsman? No words are passed between them but the teacher recognizes him in whom the seeds of wisdom have been planted.

"You must have perfect freedom — the God freedom — is that freedom I speak about. You must make your own decisions for yourself and there is only one true guide who is experienced. That is experience itself. For every ten who fail to stay on the path to God only one succeeds and some who fail are jealous, others vain and some full of malice.

"It makes no difference what decision you make, nor the course taken, you will not meet with universal favor. Though you turn to the right, or to the left, or go ahead, or turn back, there will always be a critic to advise you to the contrary.

"You are forbidden to talk even of what is known. Grudgingly, little by little, you are taught some fragments and then you are put to wearisome long tests to demonstrate that you can refrain from using what you worked so hard to get.

"All within the dualistic world is a riddle. The word two is a riddle, until you divide it into one plus one. Of every ten who tread the middle path there are nine who turn aside through avarice, though it may not be for money or passions.

"Those who tread it truly avoid vices, having found them in themselves, so that he can know their habits and is temperate in judgement, throwing no stones unless he breaks the windows of the Soul.

"Pain and pleasure are opposites of one emotion. Friendship and enmity also being opposites of one emotion, you hurt your friends and soothe your enemies. If you are sentimental you will do anything except make a fool of yourself by being sentimental.

"When you come to a decision between right and wrong, then act, do not wait on approval. If you do right, it will add no virtue to the right that friends gave their assent beforehand; rather it will give a false friend an opportunity to strengthen his attachments, so that ultimately you may listen to him to your own sorrow and undoing.

"If you do wrong it will harm you not at all for your enemies will rejoice, since proper motives will protect and preserve you in the end, and it is well to have your enemies uncovered. Be your own judge, but commit no trespass, watchfully remembering that where another's liberty begins your own inevitably meets at its borderline.

"Would you ask a musician to make inharmonies in order to teach music to you? Or must you think in terms of music before the musician's thoughts can read yours?

"The spiritual traveler is like any true musician or poet, or sculptor, for he is always trying to stir humanity. But artists can only reach people who respond to artistic impulses; others seem to look or seem to listen but art means nothing to them and they neither criticize nor praise. We breathe out our principles. There are those who have a self interest and interfer in every detail of our lives, and the first thought we have is that it is an act of God.

"You may notice that in the earth plane benevolence and altruism and the spirit of inquiry are increasing in quantity as quality. This is because it makes no difference — whatever a man's religion or his politics may be, a principle is universal, and whoever comprehends and begins to live by this principle will presently burst the bonds of his religion or politics, exactly as a tree root bursts the rocks in which it grows.

"Every man goes forward on his own responsibility. There is no escape from it. Since no two men think quite alike, there is always independent judgement. The travelers never interfer with anyone unless he reaches out to them.

"They prefer to guide valor and integrity and character into the proper spiritual channels. But how can this be done unless the individual is willing to be guided? The teacher is like a musician who plays harmonies for you to follow if you can, and just as Beethoven could not compromise with those who didn't understand him, who detested his music, neither can the traveler compromise. It is for you, or for anyone else, to agree or not as you see fit.

"The traveler hardly forsees anything in the earth world, for he is aware that all is now, in the instant of eternity. He never looks for anything in the future, never prophesizes, no more than a musician foresees the effect of music on an audience. He merely plays the harmonies, and emotion does the rest. True music, like the Bani, appeals to the inner emotion more than ever; it stirs the spirit in man that catches the inspiration. And the power which I have taught you to use is many times more subtle than the rarest music. Let it only reach man in a moment when his finest thoughts are active and it will rend the veil between him and his own reality. Then he will do the right thing always.

"I tell you nothing matters to you except what you think and what you do to others. If you expect to win praise for what you do and adulation in return for

160

what you think, you may as well give up doing and thinking, because the world will only praise what pleases it, and will only tolerate what does not cause it the necessity to think. It stifles thought with ostracism and with bayonets and then flatters itself how wise it is.

"You must learn not to discuss the teacher with others. Not that it injuries him in anyway, but gossip is a rolling stone that runs downhill. Many a man who was climbing uphill has been hit by that stone and discouraged. Some who were nearer the bottom where the stone has more impetus, are crushed.

"Before you leave, I wish to ask one question," he smiled gently. "How wise are you?"

I shook my head. "I do not know," I replied.

CHAPTER 12

The Tiger's Fang

The road back is often more difficult than the way to the Kingdom of God.

The understanding of life that one gains in his journey through the cosmic universe is that he never dies; his only interest is survival. And so all of this has a connection with the atoms of the universe. Everything around us is composed of atoms; myself, you and the very air you breathe.

The tiny atom has become the Tiger's Fang for it can be used either for man's benefit or his destruction. If we stop to think about this for a moment then we understand. Because atoms are so small their numbers must be exceedingly large. Under normal conditions a human being breathes about a pint of air with every breath.

This means that about sixteen times in every minute we inhale and exhale air, and that we are taking in and letting out no less than 25 billion atoms each time.

It is possible that we breathe the same atoms that all the geniuses of the earth world have breathed in their life time here. This is astounding but true, for every atom which has been in existence since the beginning of this universe is still living.

This is what we call the Living Truth.

No atom has ever been destroyed that we are aware

of. This is the genuine God power, the Truth of Truths! The science behind the science of truth, or the search for the ultimate reality. These tiny atoms are Souls, the intelligence, the power and presence from the gigantic Ocean of Love and Mercy, in the nameless region, the Anami Lok!

These atoms are given movement through the power of the Bani, the Shabda Dun, the Word of God, and through the movement of the lower powers in the dualistic world, that which we call the Kal power, they can be manifested into being — into materiality, crystallized for the external senses.

This is astounding to the minds of laymen, who think of God as the mysterious deity sitting on a throne way up there in a heaven controlling all lives by the threads of fate. Most of our ideas about religion come from the old mythological paganism of pantheism which includes the humanizing of elements.

The energy of the atom is the wonder of all. It is the power of God and nobody has yet understood what this is — not even the scientists in all their searching. Yet the mystics knew centuries ago and because of jealousy, and the lack of understanding between them and the scientists of the physical elements, nothing could be developed outside their own realm.

Also because of the persecutions brought on by the religious fanatics, it seemed to be that the mystics kept so close to themselves that nobody could understand what they were doing. They did not tell the outside world of their discoveries. They could have been murdered for letting out such controversial data to the public.

I came to one conclusion. That as long as we try to deal with all powers we are wasting time. We must stop searching, seeking and desiring for anything! Then all things will come to us!

The power of the mind is the thought power. Did

we ever get anywhere by trying to manipulate thought? Not one person out of a hundred can do this, but it is easier and more important to handle the emotions.

The emotions represent the love element in man. Therefore man must control feelings and by controlling his emotional nature he will have a clear mind and the ability to think.

The Word or Bani is the true element of the life force, the little atoms which spin within us, which is the control of this particle. This is truth, the essence of God. We control it via the emotional body, and not the mind, because the emotional body is the middle body of man — that which stands between the physical and the mental as the balance. The middle way which Buddha talked about, the elemental force of Christianity; the devotion that Mohammed demanded of his people, and the music that Guru Nanak, Tulsi Das, Hafiz and Rumi, as well as Shamus-i-Tabriz have filled their poetry with, and all religions use as the cardinal element of their teachings.

The masters on the path of Eckankar all have strongly emphasized the realization of God. Let us analyze what has been said here of God-realization. The basic idea was that God becomes real to the devotee, so that he can sing. "I know the one God, the omnipotent Father!"

When you come to a true teacher, it is his responsibility to make you see God and hear God. If he cannot do this then keep seeking for he has not fulfilled the requirements of a true teacher. No man can know God until he has consciously realized God. Anything short of this is more or less speculative, imaginary, visionary and imperfect.

One more point on this subject. Churches, formal religions, cults, and groups advertising themselves as mystery schools belong to the immature period of human thought and evolution which, we might say, is the childhood of the race of people on earth.

I love the Chinese philosophies because of a certain element of delicacy and mystery about them — but on the other hand most of them are dead schools of thought today. Anyone who enters a house of worship anywhere in times like these, carrying a high vibration, can feel the deadness suddenly descending upon them like a weight against the spirit, and it holds Soul in a deadly vice.

The individual must be free. This is one thing which the teacher recognizes in all men. He never informs, instructs or points out anything differently, but sends his messages to others by wave lengths.

When I became aware of the environment again Rebazar Tarzs and I were sitting in a small inn in an ancient little town in Persia that looked like a place out of a Biblical scene.

The surroundings were hot, dirty and filled with dust. The people were small in stature, undernourished and quarrelsome. It was the thirteenth century and none of these people looked as though they would make spiritual history.

This was a world on the past time track, drawn back by Rebazar Tarzs in order to let me see what the Persian mystics had to contend with. I could feel the excitement pounding within me.

A slender, grizzly bearded man in a gray turban and robe strolled into the inn. His dark, penetrating eyes started at Rebazar Tarzs. He smiled, as he crossed the room to greet the Tibetan.

"Jalalu'd-Din Rumi," said Rebazar Tarzs simply introducing the strange, mystical Persian poet of the thirteenth century.

"Wine for thee," said Rumi in a melodious voice. "Drink up!"

The Tibetan and I ordered goat's milk instead.

Startled, the great poet stared at us for a moment with a penetrating gaze. "Every man to his state," he said finally. "But I don't know how you stomach it."

"Where are we?" I asked.

"Shiraz," Rumi replied. "One of the greatest centers of culture known to the world in its day, but has now fallen into disuse and ruin. During my time the poem was developed to its finest art, in this city. On an occasion one of my poems was read to the Prince of Shiraz who fell into such ecstasy that he rent his clothes shouting 'If only I could have written that.'

"The poem was used to develop the expression of glory and love of God. I loved God so dearly that I wrote 26,000 couplets in one work alone. This is called the 'Masnavi' which is arranged in six parts or books dealing with the mystic side of the Sufi philosophy. All are in a series of stories having spiritual maxims and interpretations. It can be compared with the Book of Proverbs and the other books of the old Bible.

"One of the books is called the 'Song of the Reed' and it is the Soul's song of its love for God, and longing to be reunited with Him. It is the keynote of the 'Masnavi.'

"Do you know how long it took me to write this volume? Thirty years of work both day and night, and besides that, with my teaching of hundreds of devotees, I was the professor of philosophy and law in four different colleges, in the Quran, at the same time.

"It wasn't work. It was pleasure. God's work is never labor, but that which is done by the Soul for the purpose of becoming one in that divine bliss again.

"Man must live with understanding. This is not an emotion to be dissected by the physical scientists, but the expression of thousands of yearnings in the past lives of each man.

167

"Now I will give you a story which will illustrate a man's love for God.

"Many centuries ago there lived in this town, then a village, under the mongol rulers of Asia, a shoemaker who believed that he had a great love for God. He always boasted that others were not as great as himself, for God always talked with him. This is a strange habit of those who have never seen God, or have never known Him. They always boast of their ability to talk with the Almighty Father like we talk here at the table.

"This man grew bolder in his boasting. For the reason that nothing happened to him. God did not come to him during meditation and tell him differently, nor did he receive any punishment for it. But his great talk was gaining business for him because everybody wanted shoes made by the Holy Man, which he became known as, the "Holy Cobbler!"

"The prince of Shiraz was a true devotee of God, and loved him dearly. He meditated regularly and wanted to walk in the path of the light. He ruled his kingdom wisely, but was disturbed by this talk of the cobbler that kept reaching his ears. So one day he dressed himself in a commoner's clothes and called upon the cobbler to order a pair of shoes.

"During his discussion about the shoes, the Prince asked the cobbler about God.

"'Ah yes,' the cobbler said in a tone that rang with contempt of a superior person. 'God comes every night and tells me what to do. And sir, you know he often asks my advice on the problems of heaven.'

"This prince wondered at this, and during his meditation that night, the Lord of Lords appeared. 'Prince,' He said, 'I am the Lord of All. You have been faithful and fulfilled all obligations here on earth, but now that you have a short time left there is one thing that you can do to assure your entrance into heaven!'

"The prince said, 'I am your servant, O Lord!'

"'You are too humble, my son. This trait must be balanced within you. I am going to give you an opportunity to do so. You are to go into the forest and seek for a tiger and upon finding its lair go to the boastful cobbler of this town and order him to seek out the tiger and bring back its fang. Do all in secret!'

"The prince was puzzled but joyous at the opportunity to serve the Lord. He dressed himself like a hunter and went into the forest alone, found the tiger's lair, and returned to the palace ready to carry out the Lord's plan. He sent for the boastful cobbler and ordered him to get the tiger's fang.

"The cobbler trembled like a leaf but knew it was death in either case, but decided to risk trying to get the fang. That night he sought out the lair, found the tiger asleep and tried to kill it with a knife. But he failed and only aroused the beast and got back to the village barely ahead of the furious cat.

"Just before reaching the village limits he fell from exhaustion and awaited the attack of the tiger. Instead the Lord appeared to him. 'Boastful one,' said the Lord. 'You have failed me! While I let you talk of knowing me intimately you have failed me with the Prince. He will now kill you!'

"'What shall I do O Lord?'

"'Go back to the prince and tell him that you could not capture the tiger and pull the fang. That is all!'

"The cobbler went to the palace, ready to die, but as he entered the courtyard he kicked an object in the dust. It was found to be a tiger's fang, old and half-decayed. A cunning plan entered his mind and he took it into the palace and presented it to the prince.

"The prince recognized it as a play object belonging to his children. He was outraged but could do nothing for the cobbler had returned with a tiger's fang and a story that God had sent him to the prince.

"He was dismissed and went back to his shop a chastised man knowing that God had given him the lesson he needed in his life. However, the prince suddenly became boastful telling all that he was intimate with God and talked nightly with Him. The cobbler never again said anything that sounded like the person he was before this occurrence.

"The moral of this story is that one should first pull the tiger's fang before telling the world that he is the killer of tigers.

"This is true of all the seekers of God in the earth realm today. They boast of their intimate knowledge of God, and so far haven't even found a part of Him; not even an old decayed tiger's fang which would indicate they even knew the tiger existed.

"Filled with platitudes and boasting, the priestcraft, philosophers, scientists and metaphysicians are telling the world that their knowledge of God is greater than their fellow men.

"They are unadulterated liars. I say this without hesitation, and stand ready to back up my statement. Ask any of them if they know what the Bani, the Word of God is? Ask if they have seen the light? Ask if they know the realization of God?

"The whole pack of them will start spouting something they have read in the scriptures and this is what makes one annoyed at most of those in the category just named. They quote Jesus as their authority and scream about His love for each of them personally. None of which is true!

"The real Jesus never had any of the hocus pocus surrounding Him as the followers 2000 years hence have tried to make of his character.

"Jesus was a man, a real man! None of those pallid, pale, professional money grubbers of the earth world today would understand His message if he should suddenly appear among them.

"Call Him anything you like. Love, the Christ Consciousness, the Nazarene, the Logos, the Bread of Life, but it makes no difference. He is anything that you can think of and more too. However, do not put Him in a special category, for all saviours and prophets who came to earth to help mankind did their part and passed on to the glory of the heavenly kingdom.

"The only thing wrong in the followers of a saviour is that the majority of his followers are ready to fight you to death if you so much as say one thing against him. All saviours are great because of their union with God. All saviors have a disregard for opinionated men, and are known to shun them completely.

"What does a saint care about the opinions of others? Nothing except when others begin to get so fanatical about him that they try to own him body and Soul.

"He leaves them alone and goes elsewhere where people treat him like a fellow being. Saints do not want worship, nor the love which will own them outright. They want to keep balanced and never even enter into trite or conventional conversation about God. A saint is capable of talking about the world without any explicit reference to God, in such a way that his statement gives greater glory to God and arouses a greater love for God than the observations of someone less holy, who has to strain himself to make a connection between men and God through a lot of hackney analogies and metaphors that are so feeble that they make us think there is something wrong with their faith in their religion.

"Until man comes to the point of being a channel for God the world will be filled with contradictions. The things he loves and creates are only toys compared to the true love of the Supreme Being. When we think there is joy in the toys, the emotion turns to sorrow; and just when they are beginning to please, the pleasure turns to pain.

"Any lover of God is the conscious co-worker of the divine plan and speaks as inspired by God, because God works through man as the extreme polarity. This is like the power from the powerhouse that works through the connected light switch in the house, but the switch is neither the power nor the powerhouse. Similarly God works through each of us, especially if we are allowing ourselves to be channels for spirit — but strictly speaking we are not God Itself in a matter of words. Only the state of consciousness is God, in the pure sense. To assert oneself as God, is, strictly speaking, misguiding.

"Christ taught, 'Not of myself, but the Father (spirit) within me does these things.' If however, one says he is God, then he can be God for God is all and everywhere. The creation is an expression of God so whosoever is addressing anything in the universe is none but God Himself speaking and He is speaking to Himself.

"So long as one is in the body consciousness he may see God working through himself. If, however, he rises into God-consciousness and returns to the body consciousness he may feel that he and God are one.

"Christ stated that 'I and my Father are one.' If one remains constantly in Godhood how can he say he is God? And to whom.... as all creation is God Himself? Listening to the sayings of a Saint for a long time and loving him is a helpful factor. We may say we love the spiritual travelers but must keep the commandments to prove it, which means we cannot enter into the kingdom until we are born anew.

"A man who has developed in a certain way while in a lifetime will remain in that stage of development

172

and progress after physical death. But he who has not developed while living in the body, although loving the holy ones, will develop during his stay in the other worlds but must come back to do it again. This is true because the teachings are purely a practical subject of knowing self by self-analysis. The travelers do not hold out hollow promises to their devotees. They always tell them to attain God in a lifetime, for if you do not attain God in this life, where is the proof that you will achieve it after this life? While living in the flesh you can develop the God consciousness. This is the golden opportunity so make the best of it.

"The travelers work under the direction of God directly and assist, rather than show, souls the way back to God. God works through the saints and travelers to carry on His work through the many planes of the cosmic worlds. There are other poles through which He works but the travelers have full and direct relationship with Him and work at His call in full consciousness. There are two categories; those who work in full consciousness like the travelers, and those who get some God intoxication and carry out a plan of their own which they believe is in accord with that of the divine power.

"Sink the ego and sit in accord with all the glory of God. Can man do this?"

A fight between two, wild shaggy men interrupted the words flowing from Rumi. He looked up and watched them tumbling about the floor of the Inn. Smiling he said, "Let them fight, Let them kill one another. That is their free will and their burden and not for us to interfere unless we take upon ourselves a part of their karma. Not that we should never feel the lack of sympathy but never invite yourself to take the burden of another."

A robed man appeared in the door and called to

Rumi. "The prince is calling for you, sire. He wants to hear the Word of God spoken from your lips."

"I go now, for the unwise calls to hear the wise," Rumi remarked dryly. He got up and walked out of the Inn leaving Rebazar Tarzs and me watching the fight on the floor.

Then the Tibetan arose and left with me following.

We stood for a short time on the edge of the world talking.

He said, "Few there are who can know God and Guru. God is all and the extent of His omnipotence cannot be measured. He resides in man as spirit, and is always present in him, does all His work invisibly and unseen at all moments of day and night. Little knows the recipient how God does all that and still longs to see Him and be with Him at all times.

"Very fortunate are those who realize and see that Truth, that Godlike quality blossoming in themselves, is from a perennial source which is invisible and at the same time visible in the spiritual traveler, in the form of the teacher. The teacher is the first to recognize the potential in the chela and the chela finds himself germinating in spirit. This is the divine law that few hint at, but few ever know. The opening for spirit to manifest always manifests spirit. Rembember all that I have told you!

"Fortunate are they who become the smallest tool in helping with God's own work!

"I am always with you!"

We stepped into the boat at the shore of that bright cosmic sea and I took a seat while Rebazar Tarzs took the tiller. We went scooting over the waves to the tune of a spanking breeze, over the sparkling waves of millions of tiny atoms of Souls, to where we started this journey.

This is all that I have to tell you. Many of the details have been left out... not purposely for there

174

is not room nor the vocabulary to express that experience.

This was my experience!

This point was strong on my mind when the far shore came into sight, where the waves lashed the sandy beach.

We left the boat here.

The Tibetan lama and I started walking up the beach together.

We have never parted.

Suggested introductory books published by IWP
on ECKANKAR, the most ancient spiritual
teaching in all the universes...

THE FLUTE OF GOD (Psychology of Spirit)
ECKANKAR, THE KEY TO SECRET WORLDS
(Basic text)
THE TIGER'S FANG
(An understanding of levels of heaven)
LETTERS TO GAIL, VOL. I (Basic text)
THE SPIRITUAL NOTEBOOK
(History of ECKANKAR)
STRANGER BY THE RIVER
(Love and wisdom of the ages)
HERBS, THE MAGIC HEALERS
IN MY SOUL, I AM FREE
(Biography on Sri Paul Twitchell by Brad Steiger)

YOUR RIGHT TO KNOW
(Compilation of articles on contemporary subjects)

For more information about ECKANKAR, write:

ECKANKAR
PO Box 3100
Menlo Park, CA 94025

For a free book catalog, write:

Illuminated Way Press
PO Box 2449
Menlo Park, CA 94025